Divorce
in New Mexico

The Legal Process,
Your Rights, and What to Expect

Sandra Morgan Little, Esq.
Jan Gilman-Tepper, Esq.
Roberta S. Batley, Esq.
Tiffany Oliver Leigh, Esq.

Addicus Books
Omaha, Nebraska

An Addicus Nonfiction Book

ISBN 978-1-940495-69-9

Typography Jack Kusler

This book is not intended to serve as a substitute for an attorney. Nor is it the authors' intent to give legal advice contrary to that of an attorney.

Library of Congress Cataloging-in-Publication Data

Divorce in New Mexico : the legal process, your rights, and what to expect / Sandra Morgan Little, Jan Gilman-Tepper, Roberta S. Batley, Tiffany Oliver Leigh.
    pages cm. — (Divorce in)
  Includes index.
   ISBN 978-1-940495-69-9 (paperback)
1. Divorce—Law and legislation—New Mexico. 2. Divorce suits—New Mexico. 3. Domestic relations—New Mexico. I. Little, Sandra Morgan, author. II. Gilman-Tepper, Jan, – author. III. Batley, Roberta S., – author.
  KFN3700.D58 2015
  346.78901'66—dc23

                                                2015007616

Addicus Books, Inc.
P.O. Box 45327
Omaha, Nebraska 68145
www.AddicusBooks.com
Printed in the United States of America
10 9 8 7 6 5 4 3 2 1

To our clients. For their courage and generosity of spirit,
which inspire and teach us every day, we are grateful.

Contents

Acknowledgments

Our first acknowledgment goes to our clients. Each day they trust us to guide them through a confusing and uncertain time of their lives. They are willing to be courageous, truthful, and vulnerable, teaching us what goes on in the minds and hearts of people experiencing divorce. We are so grateful.

We thank our publishers, Rod Colvin and Jack Kusler of Addicus Books. Their enduring support made it possible for our work to benefit people all across our state.

Members of the family law and collaborative divorce bar in New Mexico have contributed more to this book than they realize. Their depth of knowledge and commitment to excellence both taught and inspired us. Special thanks go to our New Mexico judges, who every day enforce our laws and help our clients through one of the most challenging times in their lives.

We are wholly dedicated to searching for the best practices to support our clients and make the process of divorce easier for them. Much of what you see in this book is due to their working with us attorneys over the years.

If this book empowers readers on the divorce journey as we hope, it is only because of the generosity of so many, for which we extend our heartfelt gratitude.

Introduction

We are four women attorneys who see men and women every day caught up in the whirlpool of a divorce. If you are thinking about divorce, be ready for a change in every single part of your life. Parenting, family relationships, finances, social networks, personal belongings, the house, job performance—all are impacted. Your personal world will be turned upside down. There has long been a need for a reference, written in plain English, from which those who are divorcing can get answers about how the divorce process works in New Mexico. Our purpose in writing *Divorce in New Mexico* is to help you navigate through the process and ease your uncertainty.

All of our clients courageously make tough decisions throughout their divorce process as their world changes around them. Your divorce can be a growth and transformative opportunity. Having good support around you, whether it is your own therapist, your family, and/or friends, can make all the difference. Divorce adjustment groups or parenting classes can help you and your family reach a new understanding and plan for the future. *Divorce in New Mexico* is written to be a part of helping you move through this time of transition with more clarity and ease. It is not intended to be a substitute for advice from your attorney. Rather, it is designed to assist you in partnering with your attorney to reach your goals in the resolution of your divorce.

Knowledge is power. We want to explain each step in the divorce process and empower you to make sound decisions when you are facing challenging choices.

Use this book to help you know what questions to ask your attorney, to clarify difficult concepts, and to help you see the new big picture of your future.

Although every divorce is unique and circumstances can vary, we hope that *Divorce in New Mexico* will help to answer your many questions as you begin to travel the road toward a new beginning. We hope this book will also be used by professionals who support you, such as attorneys, mediators, therapists, clergy, financial advisers, and coaches.

During your divorce you will have hard, grief-filled days and you may face mountains of uncertainty, but you will get through this. In the end, you will inevitably find some relief in letting go of old sadness. You'll begin to have glimmers of hope in recreating yourself and a sure sense of new possibilities for your future.

Sandra Morgan Little, Esq.
Jan Gilman-Tepper, Esq.
Roberta S. Batley, Esq.
Tiffany Oliver Leigh, Esq.

1

Understanding the Divorce Process

At a time when your life can feel like it's in utter chaos, sometimes the smallest bit of predictability can bring a sense of comfort. The outcome of many aspects of your divorce may be unknown, increasing your fear and anxiety. But there is one part of your divorce that does have some measure of predictability and that is the divorce process itself.

Most divorces proceed in a step-by-step manner. Despite the uniqueness of your divorce, you can generally count on one phase of your divorce following the next. Sometimes just realizing that you are completing stages and moving forward with your divorce can reassure you that it won't go on forever.

It is essential to develop a basic understanding of the divorce process. This will lower your anxiety when your attorney starts talking about "depositions" or "going to trial." It can reduce your frustration about the length of the process because you understand why each step is needed. It will support you as you begin preparing for what comes next. Most importantly, understanding the divorce process will make your experience of the entire divorce easier. Who wouldn't prefer that?

1.1   What is my first step in getting a divorce?

Find a law firm that handles divorces as a regular part of its law practice. Look for a New Mexico board-certified family law specialist or get a recommendation from people who have knowledge of an attorney's experience and reputation.

Even if you are not ready to file for divorce, call to schedule a consultation with an attorney right away to obtain information about protecting yourself and your children. Even if you are not planning to file for divorce yourself, your spouse might be.

Ask the attorney what documents you should take to your initial consultation. Make a list of your questions to bring to your first meeting. Start making plans for how you will pay your attorney to begin work on your case.

1.2   Must I have an attorney to get a divorce in New Mexico?

You are not required to have an attorney to obtain a divorce in New Mexico. However, if your case involves children, alimony, significant property, retirement, or debts, you should avoid proceeding on your own.

If your divorce does not involve any of these issues, call your county courthouse to see whether or not there is a self-help desk available to provide assistance. A person who proceeds in a legal matter without an attorney is referred to as being *pro se* (on one's own).

If you are considering proceeding without an attorney, at a minimum it is a good idea to have an initial consultation with an attorney to discuss your rights and duties under the law. You may have certain rights or obligations of which you are unaware. Meeting with an attorney can help you decide whether or not to proceed on your own. It is often said that if your divorce will involve the division of retirement assets, such as state or federal retirement benefits, military pensions, or 401(k) accounts, you should have an attorney to assist you.

Also you should seek the help of an attorney if:
- You will need to sell a house or other real estate.
- There is a claim about certain property being separate or partially separate property
- There is a claim for spousal support (also known as *alimony*)
- There is a bankruptcy or potential for bankruptcy
- There is a business that will need to be valued
- There is property or a business in other states
- There are complex or difficult tax issues
- There are custody disputes.

1.3   What steps are taken during the divorce process?

The steps taken to obtain a divorce in New Mexico typically include:

- Obtain a referral for an attorney.
- Schedule an appointment with an attorney.
- Prepare questions and gather needed documents for the initial consultation.
- Meet for the initial consultation with attorney.
- Pay retainer to attorney and sign retainer agreement.
- Provide requested information and documents to your attorney.
- Choose which process you want for your divorce: mediation, negotiation, collaborative, or litigation.
    - If you choose mediation, both you and your spouse will meet with a mediator who may or may not be an attorney. You will have a series of joint sessions with the mediator to reach an agreement on all issues related to the divorce. When you and your spouse reach an agreement, one of your attorneys will draft the agreement. Your individual attorneys will review it to make sure it protects you and make the necessary changes before you sign it.
    - Negotiations begin regarding terms of a temporary order on matters such as custody, support, and temporary possession of the family home.
    - If you select the collaborative process, you and your spouse will each select a collaboratively trained attorney to represent you. There will be other members of the collaborative team as well. A financial neutral member will gather all the financial information and help prepare a property and debt work sheet and a child-support work sheet, and will recommend an appropriate settlement based upon the interest for each of the spouses. A divorce coach, who is a mental health professional, will help each spouse navigate the divorce process. A child specialist will help them

work out and draft a parenting plan that will best fit their children.

- ■ If you select a process where you are in litigation, motions will be filed on various issues, discovery will probably be done, and you may have a trial before a judge to determine some or all the issues. It is rare that all issues in a divorce are tried before the judge. Spouses usually have agreed on only some issues and request the court to decide the ones they could not agree upon.

- Take other actions as advised by attorney.
- Attorney prepares petition for dissolution of marriage (divorce) and supporting documents for your review and signature.
- Attorney files petition for dissolution of marriage with clerk of the court. A temporary domestic order (TDO) is immediately entered by the court. The TDO is to keep the financial and custodial status quo in place.
- Attorney may request a hearing before the court to address temporary matters.
- Attorneys prepare financial work sheets for interim hearing.
- A temporary hearing is held.

OR

- Parties reach an agreement on temporary matters.
- A temporary order is prepared by one attorney, approved by other attorney, and submitted to the judge for signature.
- If there are minor children, parties may be required to attend a parent education class, develop a parenting plan, or have a hearing before the court concerning temporary custody.
- Both sides conduct discovery to obtain information regarding all relevant facts. If needed, obtain valuations of all assets, including expert opinions.
- Confer with attorney to review facts, identify issues, assess strengths and weaknesses of case, review strategy, and develop proposal for settlement.

- Spouses, guided by their attorneys, attempt to reach an agreement through written proposals, mediation, settlement conferences, or other negotiation.
- Parties reach an agreement on all issues.
- Attorney prepares a final decree of dissolution of marriage and required supporting court orders for approval by spouses and attorneys.

OR

- If you are in the collaborative process, all the necessary financial documents are exchanged between the parties. The financial neutral reviews them and prepares an asset-and-liability work sheet in order to consider an agreement.
- If there are children, the child specialist works with the spouses and their children to work out an age-appropriate parenting plan.
- Meetings are conducted with the spouses, financial neutral, divorce coach, and child specialist to come to a tailor-made agreement for the spouses and their children.
- The attorney requests a trial setting for the court to set a trial date.
- Pay trial retainer to fund the work needed to prepare for trial and services for the day(s) of trial.
- Parties prepare for trial on unresolved issues.

OR

- Trial preparations proceed and include the preparation of witnesses, trial exhibits, legal research on contested issues, pretrial motions, trial brief, preparation of direct and cross-examination of witnesses, preparation of opening statement, subpoena of witnesses, and closing argument to the court.
- Meet with attorney for final trial preparation.
- A trial is held.
- The judge makes a decision.
- Attorney prepares final decree of dissolution of marriage.

- Other attorney approves final decree of dissolution of marriage, or a hearing is required for the judge to decide on the language in the final decree of dissolution of marriage.
- Final decree of dissolution of marriage is submitted to judge for signature.
- The judge signs final decree of dissolution of marriage.
- Make payments and sign documents (deeds or titles) pursuant to final decree of dissolution of marriage.
- Prepare documents required to divide retirement accounts and ensure the payment of child support are submitted to the court.
- Pay any remaining balance due on attorney's fees or receive refund.

1.4   Is New Mexico a *no-fault* state, or do I need grounds for a divorce?

New Mexico, like most states, is a no-fault divorce state. This means that neither you nor your spouse is required to prove that the other is "at fault" in order to be granted a divorce. Factors such as infidelity, cruelty, or abandonment are not necessary to receive a divorce in New Mexico, and none of those grounds will result in an unequal division of assets or payment of money. Rather, it is necessary to prove that "the legitimate ends of the marriage relationship are destroyed, preventing any reasonable expectation of reconciliation" (for example, there is no possibility of reconciliation between you and your spouse).

The testimony of either you or your spouse that you do not wish to continue to be married is sufficient evidence for the court to rule that the marriage should be dissolved.

1.5   How will a judge view my infidelity or my spouse's infidelity?

Because New Mexico is a no-fault divorce state, a judge generally will not consider either party's infidelity to be relevant. The exception is that if, rather than filing for a divorce on no-fault grounds, you choose to file on the grounds of infidelity, you must be able to prove such infidelity.

1.6 Do I have to get divorced in the same state in which I married?

No. Regardless of where you were married, you may seek a divorce in New Mexico if the jurisdictional requirements of residency are met. The jurisdictional requirements are discussed in the following question.

1.7 How long must I have lived in New Mexico to get a divorce in the state?

Either you or your spouse must have been a resident of New Mexico for at least six months to meet the residency requirement for a divorce in New Mexico. If neither party meets the residency requirement, other legal options are available for your protection.

If you do not meet the six-month residency requirement, talk to your attorney about options such as a legal separation or a protection order.

1.8 My spouse has told me she will never "give" me a divorce. Can I get one in New Mexico anyway?

Yes. New Mexico does not require that your spouse agree to a divorce. If your spouse threatens to not "give" you a divorce, know that in New Mexico this is an idle threat without any basis in the law.

Under New Mexico law, to obtain a divorce you must be able to prove that "the legitimate ends of the marriage relationship are destroyed, preventing any reasonable expectation of reconciliation." It is not necessary to have your spouse agree to the divorce or to allege the specific difficulties that arose during the marriage to obtain a divorce in New Mexico.

1.9 Can I divorce my spouse in New Mexico if he or she lives in another state?

Provided you have met the residency requirements for living in New Mexico for six months, you can file for divorce here even if your spouse lives in another state. However, the New

Mexico court may not have the jurisdiction to divide property or debt, or award custody or support.

Discuss with your attorney the facts that will need to be proven and the necessary steps to give your spouse proper notice to ensure that the court will have jurisdiction over your spouse. Your attorney can counsel you on whether or not it is possible to proceed with the divorce.

1.10 Can I get a divorce even when I don't know where my spouse is currently living?

New Mexico law allows you to proceed with a divorce even if you do not know the current address of your spouse. First, take action to attempt to locate your spouse. Contact family members, friends, former coworkers, or anyone else who might know your spouse's whereabouts. Utilize resources on the Internet that are designed to help locate people.

Let your attorney know of the efforts you have made to attempt to find your spouse. Inform your attorney of your spouse's last known address, as well as any work address or other address where this person may be found. Once your attorney attempts to give notice to your spouse without success, it is possible to ask the court to proceed with the divorce by giving notice through publication in a newspaper.

Although your divorce may be granted following service of notice by publication in a newspaper, you may not be able to get other court orders such as those for child support or alimony without giving personal notice to your spouse. Talk to your attorney about your options and rights if you don't know where your spouse is living.

1.11 I just moved to a different county within the state of New Mexico. Do I have to file in the county where my spouse lives?

You may file your petition for dissolution of marriage either in the county where you reside or in the county where your spouse resides.

1.12   I immigrated to New Mexico. Will my immigration status stop me from getting a divorce?

If you meet the residency requirements for divorce in New Mexico, you can get a divorce here regardless of your immigration status. Talk to your immigration attorney about the likelihood of a divorce leading to immigration challenges.

If you are a victim of domestic violence, tell your attorney. You may be eligible for a change in your immigration status under the federal *Violence Against Women Act.*

1.13   I want to get divorced in my Indian tribal court. What do I need to know?

Each Indian tribal court has its own laws governing divorce. Requirements for residency; grounds for divorce; and the laws regarding property, alimony, and children can vary substantially from state law. Some tribes have very different laws governing the grounds for your divorce, removal of children from the home, and cohabitation.

Contact an attorney who is knowledgeable about the law in your tribal court for legal advice on pursuing a divorce in your tribal court or on the requirements for recording a divorce obtained in state court with the clerk of the tribal court.

1.14   Is there a waiting period for a divorce in New Mexico?

No. There is no waiting period for a divorce in New Mexico. The divorce becomes final the day the final decree of dissolution of marriage is signed by the judge and filed with the court.

1.15   What is a *divorce petition*?

A *divorce petition,* also referred to as a *petition for dissolution of marriage,* is a document signed by the person filing for divorce and filed with the clerk of the court to initiate the divorce process. The petition for dissolution of marriage will provide, in very general terms, what the petitioner is asking the court to order.

1.16 My spouse said she filed for divorce last week, but my attorney says there's nothing on file at the courthouse. What does it mean to "file for divorce"?

When attorneys use the term *filing* they are typically referring to filing a legal document at the courthouse, such as delivering a petition for dissolution of marriage to the clerk of the court. Sometimes a person who has hired an attorney to begin a divorce action uses the phrase "I've filed for divorce," although no papers have yet been taken to the courthouse to start the legal process.

1.17 If we both want a divorce, does it matter who files?

No. In the eyes of the court, the petitioner (the party who files the petition for dissolution of marriage) and the respondent (the other spouse) are not seen differently by virtue of which party filed. The court, as a neutral decision maker, will not give preference to either party. Both parties will be given adequate notice, and each will have a chance to be heard and present an argument.

1.18 Are there advantages to filing first?

It depends. Discuss with your attorney whether there are any advantages to you filing first. Your attorney may advise you to file first or to wait until your spouse files, depending upon the overall strategy for your case and your circumstances. Once you file a petition for dissolution of marriage, a temporary domestic order (TDO) will be issued and will be effective on you. It will not be effective on your spouse until two days after your spouse has been served.

Allow your attorney to support you in making the decision about whether and when to initiate the legal process by filing a petition for dissolution of marriage.

1.19 Can I stop the newspaper from publishing notice of the filing or granting of my divorce?

Documents filed with the court, such as a petition for dissolution of marriage and a final decree of dissolution of marriage, are matters of public record. Newspapers have a right to access this information, and some newspapers publish this information as a matter of routine. There is no set schedule to determine when this information will be published. Contact your local newspaper to learn more.

In rare cases, a divorce file may be kept private, referred to as being "sealed" or "under seal" if the court orders it.

1.20 Is there a way to avoid embarrassing my spouse and not have the sheriff or a process server serve him/her with the divorce papers at his/her workplace?

Talk to your attorney about the option of having your spouse sign a document known as an *acceptance of service*. The signing and filing of this document with the court can eliminate the need to have your spouse served by the sheriff.

The use of an acceptance of service document is not appropriate for all cases, so discuss with your attorney the better choice for your case.

1.21 Should I sign an acceptance of service document even if I don't agree with what my spouse has written in the petition for dissolution of marriage?

Signing the acceptance of service document does not mean that you agree with anything your spouse has stated in the petition for dissolution of marriage or anything that your spouse is asking for in the divorce.

Signing the acceptance of service document only substitutes for having the sheriff or a process server personally hand you the documents. You do not waive the right to object to anything your spouse has stated in the petition for dissolution of marriage.

Follow your attorney's advice on whether and when to sign an acceptance of service document.

1.22 Why should I contact an attorney right away if I have received divorce papers?

If your spouse has filed for divorce, it is important that you obtain legal advice as soon as possible. Even if you and your spouse are getting along, having independent legal counsel can help you make decisions now that could affect your divorce later.

After your spouse has filed for divorce, a temporary hearing can be scheduled at any time. It is possible you will receive only a few days' notice of a temporary hearing. You will be better prepared for a temporary hearing if you have already retained an attorney.

After your acceptance of service document has been filed with the court, or you have been served by the sheriff, a written answer responding to your spouse's petition for dissolution of marriage must be filed with the court within thirty days.

1.23   What is an *ex parte court order*?

An *ex parte court order* is obtained by one party going to the judge to ask for something without giving prior notice or an opportunity to be heard by the other side.

Judges are generally reluctant to sign *ex parte* orders. Ordinarily the court will require the other side to have notice of any requests for court orders, and a hearing before the judge will be held.

Ex parte orders are generally limited to emergency situations, such as requests for temporary restraining orders and protection orders.

When an *ex parte* order is granted, the party who did not request the order will have an opportunity to have a subsequent hearing within a few days before the judge to determine whether the order should remain in effect.

1.24   What is a *motion*?

A *motion* is a request that the judge enter a court order of some type. For example, your attorney may file a written motion with the court asking for an order related to temporary custody, child support, parenting time, or financial matters, such as payment of bills.

Some motions are made to handle certain procedural aspects of your case, such as a motion for a continuance asking that a court date be changed or a motion for extension of time asking that the court extend a deadline. In some cases, a motion may be made orally rather than in writing; for example, when an issue arises during the course of a court hearing or trial.

1.25 Once my petition for dissolution of marriage is filed, how soon can a temporary hearing be held to decide what happens with our child and our finances while the divorce is pending?

How soon a hearing can be held depends on the court's docket, or calendar. The court will generally schedule a temporary hearing as soon as possible after such a hearing is requested; however, depending on how busy the assigned judge is, it may be weeks or even months before the temporary hearing will occur.

1.26 How much notice will I get if my spouse seeks a temporary order?

New Mexico law requires that you receive reasonable notice of any court hearings, usually at least five days. In the case of hearings on *ex parte* motions or orders, this notice may be shortened.

1.27 During my divorce, what am I responsible for doing?

Your attorney will explain what actions you should take to further the divorce process and to help you reach the best possible outcome.

You will be asked to:

- Keep in regular contact with your attorney.
- Update your attorney regarding any changes in your contact information, such as address, phone numbers, and e-mail address.
- Provide your attorney with all requested documents.
- Provide requested information in a timely manner.
- Complete forms and questionnaires.
- Keep appointments with your attorney.
- Appear in court on time.
- Be direct about asking any questions you might have.
- Tell your attorney your thoughts on settlement or what you would like the judge to order in your case.
- Remain respectful toward your spouse throughout the process.

- Refrain from involving your children in the litigation.
- Comply with any temporary court orders, such as restraining or support orders.
- Advise your attorney of any significant developments in your case.

By doing your part in the divorce process, you enable your attorney to partner with you for a better outcome while also lowering your attorney fees.

1.28 I'm worried that I won't remember to ask my attorney about all of the issues in my case. How can I be sure I don't miss anything?

Write down all of the topics you want to discuss with your attorney, including what your goals are for the outcome of the divorce. Use the Divorce Issues Checklist below as a guide. The sooner you are able to clarify your goals, the easier it will be for your attorney to support you in obtaining what you want most. Realize that your attorney will think of some issues that you may not have thought of. Your attorney's experience will be helpful in making sure nothing important is forgotten.

Divorce Issues Checklist

Issue	Notes
Dissolution	
Custody of minor children	
Removal of children from jurisdiction	
Parenting plan	
Child support	
Deviation from child support guidelines	
Abatement of child support	
Travel expenses to facilitate parenting time for out-of-town/state parents	
Life insurance to fund unpaid child support	
Automatic withholding for support	
Child-care expenses	

Divorce Issues Checklist (Continued)

Issue	Notes
Child-care credit	
Health insurance for minor children	
Uninsured medical expenses for minor children	
Extracurricular activities	
Qualified medical support order (QMSO)	
Private school tuition for children	
College expenses for children	
College savings accounts for benefit of children	
Health insurance on the parties	
Real property: rentals, cabins, commercial property, etc.	
Time-shares	
Retirement accounts	
Federal or military pensions	
Business interests	
Bank accounts	
Investments	
Stock options	
Stock purchase plans	
Life insurance policies	
Frequent flyer miles	
Credit card points	
Season tickets for events	
Premarital or nonmarital assets	
Premartial or nonmarital debts	
Pets	

Divorce Issues Checklist (Continued)

Issue	Notes
Personal property division: including motor vehicles, recreational vehicles, campers, airplanes, collections, furniture, electronics, tools, household goods	
Exchange date for personal property	
Division of martial debt	
Property settlement	
Spousal support or alimony	
Life insurance to fund unpaid spousal support	
Tax exemptions for minor children	
IRS Form 8332	
Filing status for tax returns for last/current year	
Former name restoration	
Attorney fees	

1.29 My spouse has all of our financial information. How will I be able to prepare for negotiations and trial if I don't know the facts or have the documents?

Once your divorce has been filed with court and temporary matters have been addressed, your attorney will proceed with a process known as *discovery.*

Through discovery, your attorney can ask your spouse to provide documents and information needed to prepare your case. Your attorney can also subpoena information directly from an institution to obtain the requested documentation.

1.30 My spouse and I both want our divorce to be amicable. How can we keep it that way?

You and your spouse are to be commended for your willingness to cooperate while focusing on moving through the divorce process. This will not only make your lives easier and save you money on attorney fees, but it is also more likely to result in an outcome with which you are both satisfied. There are several options in the divorce process, and you should discuss such options with your attorney to determine the best process for you and your children.

Find an attorney who understands your goal to reach settlement and encourage your spouse to do the same. Cooperate with the prompt exchange of necessary information. Ask your attorney about the options of mediation, negotiation, and collaboration in reaching agreement. Even if you are not able to settle all of the issues in your divorce, these actions can increase the likelihood of agreement on many of the terms of your final decree of dissolution of marriage.

1.31 Can I pick my judge?

You may not pick your own judge or judge "shop." Judge shopping occurs when a person involved in a legal case attempts to influence the court's assignment of a case so that it will be directed to or away from a particular judge. Talk to your attorney about the reasons you want a different judge. If you believe that your judge has a conflict of interest, such as being a close friend of your spouse, you may have a basis for asking the judge to be recused in order to allow another judge to hear the case.

1.32 How long will it take to get my divorce?

The more you and your spouse are in agreement, the faster your divorce will conclude. Without agreement, your divorce may take several months or even years.

Assuming all issues, such as custody, support, property, and debts, are completely settled between you and your spouse, if you so choose, your attorney can prepare the necessary paperwork and file everything together.

1.33 What is the significance of my divorce being final?

Obtaining your final decree of dissolution of marriage is important for many reasons. It can affect your right to remarry, your eligibility for health insurance from your former spouse, and your filing status for income taxes.

1.34   When does my divorce become final?

Your divorce is final on the date that the final decree of dissolution of marriage is entered by the court. In most cases, this will be the same day the judge signs the final decree of dissolution of marriage. This is your date of divorce.

1.35   Can I start using my former name right away and how do I get my name legally restored?

You may begin using your former name at any time, provided you are not doing so for any unlawful purpose, such as to avoid your creditors. Many agencies and institutions, however, will not alter their records without a court order changing your name.

If you want your former name restored, let your attorney know this early on so that this provision can be included in your final decree of dissolution of marriage. If you want to change your legal name after the divorce and have not provided for it in your final decree of dissolution of marriage, it will be necessary for you to undergo a separate legal action for a name change.

2

Coping with Stress during the Divorce Process

It may have been a few years ago. Or, it may have been many years ago. Perhaps it was only months. But, when you said "I do," you meant it. Like most people getting married, you planned to be a happily married couple for life.

But things happen. Life brings change. People change. Whatever the circumstance, you now find yourself considering divorce. The emotions of divorce run from one extreme to another as you journey through the process. You may feel relief and ready to move on with your life. On the other hand, you may feel emotions that are quite painful: anger, fear, sorrow, a deep sense of loss or failure. Remember, it is important to find support for coping with all of these strong emotions.

Because going through a divorce can be an emotional time, having a clear understanding of the divorce process and what to expect will help you make better decisions. And, when it comes to decision making, search inside yourself to clarify your intentions and goals for the future. Let these intentions be your guide.

Take a moment to think about what your personal/individual goals are for this divorce. What is most important to you? Make a list of your top five goals. Many of our clients have shared their lists with us and they seem to almost universally include:

- I want my children to be okay.
- I want to have as much financial security as possible.

- I want the process we choose to be as efficient and concluded as soon as possible.
- I want to keep attorney's fees to a minimum.
- I would like to end the relationship with my spouse in a manner so we can stand to be in the same room together in the future for events such as our children's graduations, weddings, and births of grandchildren.

Now, having thought through your primary goals, every time you are asked to make a decision, check your choices against these individual goals. Does "X" choice further your goals? If not, don't make that choice.

2.1 My spouse left home weeks ago. I don't want a divorce because I feel our marriage can be saved. Should I still see an attorney?

It's a good idea to see an attorney. Whether you want a divorce or not, there may be important actions for you to take now to protect your assets, credit, home, children, and future right to support. In question 1.2, we discussed the times when it is really important for you to have an attorney assist in your legal representation.

It is best to be prepared with the support of an attorney, even if you decide not to file for a divorce at this time. If your spouse files for divorce, a temporary hearing could be heard in just a matter of days.

2.2 The thought of going to an attorney's office to talk about divorce is more than I can bear. I canceled the first appointment I made because I just couldn't do it. What should I do?

Many people going through a divorce are dealing with attorneys for the first time and feel anxious about the experience. Ask a trusted friend or family member to help you prepare for your meeting. He or she can support you by writing down your questions in advance and making sure you are comfortable before going into the consultation. Though many people want to have friends with them in a consultation, this is discouraged as the communications between you and your attorney are protected by the "attorney–client privilege" which assures that what you say in confidence to your attorney generally cannot be revealed to anyone else. By allowing a third party to hear all the details that you are discussing with your attorney, you are essentially waiving this privilege and this could hurt you in the litigation.

Nothing bad is going to happen at a consultation with an attorney. The attorney is there to hear your story and advise you about the legal realities facing you. This cannot hurt you, and might very well help you. It is very likely that you will feel greatly relieved just to be better informed after the meeting.

2.3   There is some information about my marriage that I think my attorney needs, but I'm too embarrassed to discuss it. Must I tell the attorney?

What your attorney does not know may be used by your spouse's attorney to hurt you. Your attorney has an ethical duty to maintain confidentiality. Past events in your marriage are matters that your attorney is obligated to keep private, unless you agree to the disclosure of the information. Particularly if something is likely to be brought up by your spouse in the litigation, it is much better that your attorney know about it in advance. Attorneys who practice divorce law are accustomed to hearing intimate information about families. Although it is deeply personal to you, it is unlikely that anything you tell your attorney will be a shock, and it may not even be relevant to your case.

It may feel uncomfortable for a short moment, but it is important that your attorney has complete information so that your interests can be fully protected. If speaking directly about these facts still seems too hard, consider putting them in a letter to your attorney.

2.4   I'm unsure about how to tell our children about the divorce, and I'm worried I'll say the wrong thing. What's the best way?

How you talk to your children about the divorce will depend upon their ages, level of maturity, and development. Changes in your children's everyday lives, such as a change of residence or one parent leaving the home, are very important to them. Information about legal proceedings and meetings with attorneys are best kept among adults.

Simpler answers are best for young children. Avoid giving them more information than they need. Use the adults in your life as a source of support to meet your own emotional needs.

After the initial discussion, keep the door open to further talks with your children by creating opportunities for them to talk about the divorce. Use these times to acknowledge their feelings and offer support. Always assure them that the divorce is not their fault and that they are still loved by both you and your spouse, regardless of the divorce.

2.5   My youngest child seems very depressed about the divorce, the middle one is angry, and my teenager is skipping school. How can I cope?

A child's reaction to divorce can vary depending upon his/her age and other factors. Some may cry and beg for reconciliation, and others may behave inappropriately. Reducing conflict with your spouse, being a consistent and nurturing parent, and making sure both of you remain involved with your children are all actions that can support your children regardless of how they are reacting to the divorce.

Support groups for children whose parents are divorcing are available at many schools and religious communities. A school counselor may be able to provide some support. If more help is needed, confer with a therapist experienced in working with children.

2.6   I am so frustrated by my spouse's "Disneyland parent" behavior. Is there anything I can do to stop this?

Feelings of guilt, competition, or remorse sometimes lead a parent to be tempted to spend parenting time in trips to the toy store and special activities. Other times these feelings can result in an absence of discipline in an effort to become the favored parent or to make the time "special."

Shift your focus from the other parent's behavior to your own, and do your best to be an outstanding parent during your time with the children. You cannot control your spouse's behavior, but you can control your own. This includes keeping a routine for your children for family meals, bedtimes, chores, and homework. Encourage family activities, as well as individual time with each child, when it's possible.

During the time when a child's life is changing, providing a consistent and stable routine in your home can ease his/her anxiety and provide comfort.

2.7 Between requests for information from my spouse's attorney and my own attorney, I am totally overwhelmed. How do I manage gathering all of this detailed information by the deadlines imposed?

First, simply get started. Often, the thought about a task is worse than the job itself.

Second, break it down into smaller tasks. Perhaps one evening you gather your tax returns and on the weekend you work on your monthly living expenses.

Third, let in support. Ask that friend of yours who just loves numbers to come over for an evening with her calculator to help you get organized.

Finally, communicate with your attorney. Your attorney or a paralegal in your attorney's office may be able to make your job easier by giving you suggestions or help. It may be that essential information can be provided now and the details submitted later.

2.8 I am so depressed about my divorce that I'm having difficulty getting out of bed in the morning to care for my children. What should I do?

See your health care provider. Feelings of depression are common during a divorce. You also want to make sure that you identify any physical health concerns.

Although feelings of sadness are common during a divorce, more serious depression means it's time to seek professional support.

Your health and your ability to care for your children are both essential. Follow through on recommendations by your health care professionals for therapy, medication, or other measures to improve your wellness.

2.9   Will taking prescribed medication to help treat my insomnia and depression hurt my case?

Not necessarily. Talk to your health care professionals and follow their recommendations. Taking care of your health is of the utmost importance during this difficult time, and will serve your best interest as well as the best interest of your children. Inform your attorney of any medications that you are taking or treatment that you are seeking.

2.10   I know I need help to cope with the stress of the divorce, but I can't afford counseling. What can I do?

You are wise to recognize that divorce is a time for letting in support. You can explore a number of options, including:

- Meeting with a member of the clergy or lay chaplain.
- Joining a divorce support group.
- Turning to friends and family members.
- Going to a therapist or divorce coach. If budget is a concern, contact a social agency that offers counseling services on a sliding-fee scale.

Additionally, there are several organizations listed in Resources at the back of this book that should be consulted to help determine if low-cost counseling is available to you. If none of these options are available, look again at your budget. You may see that counseling is so important that you decide to find a way to increase your income or lower your expenses to support this investment in your well-being.

2.11   I'm the one who filed for divorce, but I still have loving feelings toward my spouse and feel sad about divorcing. Does this mean I should dismiss my divorce?

Strong feelings of caring about your spouse often persist after a divorce is filed. Whether or not to proceed with a divorce is a deeply personal decision. Although feelings can inform us of our thoughts, sometimes they can also cause us to not look at everything there is to see in our situation.

Have you and your spouse participated in marriage counseling? Has your spouse refused to seek treatment for an addiction? Are you worried about the safety of you or your children if you remain in the marriage? Can you envision yourself as financially secure if you remain in this marriage? Is your spouse involved in another relationship?

The answers to these questions can help you get clear about whether or not to consider reconciliation. Talk to your therapist, coach, or religious advisor to help determine the right path for you.

2.12   Will my attorney charge me for the time I spend talking about my feelings about my spouse and my divorce?

It depends. If you are paying your attorney by the hour, expect to be charged for the time your attorney spends talking with you. If your attorney is being paid a flat rate for handling your divorce, the time spent talking with you will be included in the fee.

2.13   My attorney doesn't seem to realize how difficult my divorce is for me. How can I get him to understand?

Everyone wants support and compassion from the professionals who help during a divorce. Speak frankly with your attorney about your concerns. It may be that your attorney does not see your concerns as being relevant to the job of getting your desired outcome in the divorce. Your willingness to improve the communication will help your attorney understand how best to support you in the process and will help you understand which matters are best left for discussion with your therapist or a supportive friend.

2.14   I've been told not to speak ill of my spouse in front of my child, but I know he/she is doing this all the time. Why can't I just speak the truth?

It can be devastating for your child to hear you bad-mouthing his/her other parent. What your child needs is permission to love both of you, regardless of any bad parental behavior. The best way to support your child during this time is to encourage a positive relationship with the other parent.

2.15 Nobody in our family has ever been divorced and I feel really ashamed. Will my children feel the same way?

Making a change in how you see your family identity is huge for you. The best way to help your children is to establish a sense of pride in their new family and to look forward to the future with a real sense of possibility.

Your children will have an opportunity to witness you overcoming obstacles, demonstrating independence, and moving forward in your life notwithstanding challenges. You can be a great teacher to them during this time by demonstrating pride in your family and in yourself.

2.16 I am terrified of having my deposition taken. My spouse's attorney is very aggressive, and I'm afraid I'm going to say something that will hurt my case.

A deposition is an opportunity for your spouse's attorney to gather information and to assess the type of witness you will be if the case proceeds to trial. Feeling anxious about your deposition is normal. However, regardless of the personality of the attorneys, most depositions in divorces are quite uneventful.

Remember that your attorney will be seated by your side at all times to support you. Ask to meet with your attorney in advance to prepare you for the deposition. Review with your attorney all documents that might be examined at the deposition. If you are worried about specific questions that might be asked, talk to your attorney about them ahead of time. Enlist your attorney's support in being well prepared.

2.17 I am still so angry at my spouse. How can I be expected to sit in the same room during a settlement conference?

If you are still really angry at your spouse, it may be beneficial to postpone the conference for a time. You might also consider seeking some counseling to support you in coping with your feelings of anger.

Another option might be "shuttle" negotiations. With this method, you and your attorney remain in one room while your spouse and his/her attorney are in another. Settlement offers are then relayed between the attorneys throughout the negotiation process. By shifting your focus from your angry feelings to your goal of a settlement, it may be easier to proceed through the process.

2.18   I'm afraid I can't make it through court without having an emotional breakdown. How do I prepare?

A divorce trial can be a highly emotional time, calling for lots of support. Some of these ideas may help you through the process:

- Meet with your attorney or the firm's support staff in advance of your court date to prepare you for court.
- Ask you attorney whether there are any documents you should review in preparation for court, such as your deposition.
- Visit the courtroom in advance to get comfortable with the surroundings.
- Ask your attorney about having a support person with you on your court date.
- Ask yourself what is the worst thing that could happen and consider what options you would have if it did.
- Avoid alcohol, eat healthfully, exercise, and have plenty of rest during the period of time leading up to the court date. Each of these will help you to prepare for the emotions of the day.
- Plan what you intend to wear in advance. You should plan on conservative and professional clothing. Small preparations will lower your stress.
- Visualize the experience going well. Picture yourself sitting in the witness chair, giving clear, confident, and truthful answers to easy questions.
- Arrive early in the courthouse and make sure you have a plan for parking your car if you are not familiar with the area.
- Take slow, deep breaths. Breathing deeply will steady your voice, calm your nerves, and improve your focus.

Your attorney will be prepared to support you throughout the proceedings. By taking the above steps, you can increase the ease of your experience.

2.19   I am really confused. One day I think the divorce is a mistake; the next day I know I can't go back, and a few minutes later I can hardly wait to be single again. Some days I just don't believe I'm getting divorced. What's happening?

Denial, transition, and acceptance are common passages for a person going through a divorce. One moment you might feel excited about your future and a few hours later you think your life is ruined.

What can be helpful to remember is that you may not pass from one stage to the next in a direct line. Feelings of anger or sadness may well up in you long after you thought you had moved on. Similarly, your mood might feel bright as you think about your future plans, even though you still miss your spouse.

Taking good care of yourself is essential during this period of your life. What you are going through requires a tremendous amount of energy. Allow yourself to experience your emotions, but also continue moving forward with your life. These steps will help your life get easier day by day.

3

Working with Your Attorney

If there is one thing you can be sure of in your divorce, it's that you will be given plenty of advice. Well-intentioned neighbors, cousins, and complete strangers will be happy to tell you war stories about their ex or about their sister who got divorced in some other state or some other country. Many will insist they know what you should do, even though they know nothing about the facts of your case or the law in New Mexico.

But there is one person whose advice will—and should—matter to you: your attorney. Your attorney should be your trusted and supportive advocate at all times throughout your divorce, while also being the voice of reason during this emotional time. The counsel of your attorney can affect your life for years to come. A good attorney does not just tell you what you want to hear, but what you need to hear. You will never regret taking the time and energy to choose the right one for you.

You should see your relationship with your attorney as a collaborative partnership for pursuing what is most important to you and working toward your personal goals. With clear and open attorney–client communication, you will have the best outcome possible and your entire divorce will be less stressful. To enhance this open attorney–client communication, you cannot be afraid to ask questions. Asking questions is the means to clear and open communication with your attorney, which, in turn, leads to understandable, if not always agreeable, results.

By working closely with the right attorney, you can trust the professional advice you receive and simply thank the well-meaning advice givers for their concern.

3.1 Where do I begin looking for an attorney for my divorce?

There are many ways to find a divorce attorney. Most importantly, find a law firm that concentrates its practice in the area of family law. This is a very specialized area of the law and just like you would not ask a cardiologist to do brain surgery, you should not consult with an attorney who does not regularly practice in the field of family law. To start, ask people you trust—friends and family members who have gone through a divorce—if they thought they had a good attorney (or if their former spouse did). If you know professionals who work with attorneys (such as CPAs, psychologists, or appraisers), ask for a referral to an attorney who is experienced in family law.

Consult the State Bar of New Mexico (505) 797-6000 or www.nmbar.org for a referral. Be sure to specify that you are looking for an attorney who handles divorces or is a *family law specialist*. In New Mexico, an attorney can become a family law specialist based upon the amount of time their practice is dedicated to family law, the amount of time spent learning family law through continuing education, the number of years they have been practicing family law, and the recommendations of their peers and of judges. The State Bar of New Mexico website provides a list of persons that have applied for and been granted the distinction of family law specialist.

There are also certain specialty organizations for family law attorneys with strict admission standards regarding experience and ability that maintain online listings of their members. Probably the most well known and reputable of these is the American Academy of Matrimonial Attorneys (AAML), at AAML. org. The AAML is an exclusive organization that elects only accomplished and experienced family attorneys as members. On this website, you can locate the New Mexico members of the AAML.

There are other organizations that maintain directories of members who have been recognized by their peers as being outstanding in their field. The most well known is Martindale-Hubbell. This service sends out surveys to other attorneys and judges to rate attorneys. If possible, you will want to find a family law attorney who is "A/V" rated—meaning that other attorneys and judges have rated that attorney as "very high" to "preeminent" in skill, with very high ethics. The service has two main sites: Martindale.com (search for attorneys at www. martin-dale.com/Find-Lawyers-and-Law-Firms.aspx) and Lawyers.com (search for attorneys at www.lawyers.com). Another such service is Avvo, which mainly relies on a proprietary computer algorithm to rank attorneys on the basis of public information. Avvo's website and information can be found at avvo. com (search for attorneys at www.avvo.com/find-a-lawyer). In addition, organizations such as Best Lawyers (www.bestlawyers.com) and Super Lawyers (www.superlawyers.com) provide consumers with a list of attorneys recognized as outstanding in their field.

It is also helpful to go online and look at attorney websites. Generally an attorney's website will provide professional information about the attorney, but it may also contain such information as their philosophy on representation or their office policies. Our website www.lgtfamilylaw.com also provides information on different areas of family law and has extensive information about our firm and resources for potential clients.

Do remember that, as with most things on the Internet, you should take whatever you find with a grain of salt—it is possible for anyone with a grudge to post false and even defamatory information about an attorney. So, do not assume that everything you read about an attorney posted by some other person—good or bad—is necessarily true.

3.2　How do I choose the right attorney?

Choosing the right attorney for your divorce is an important decision. Your attorney should be a trusted professional with whom you feel comfortable sharing information openly. He or she should also zealously advocate on your behalf within the confines of the rules and procedures that govern attorney conduct.

You will rely upon your attorney to help you make many decisions throughout the course of your divorce. You will also entrust your legal counsel to make a range of strategic and procedural decisions on your behalf. Do not be afraid to request an explanation for any of these choices and actions.

Generally, your first meeting with your potential attorney will be a formal consultation. It is important to remember that your attorney is there not only to inform you of the law and what to expect from the legal process, but also to answer your questions about all related matters that will support your decisions. Most attorneys want to use this first meeting to "hear your story" and to fully inform you of your legal options given the limited information that they receive in this meeting.

Again, feel free to ask questions and seek all information you need to help you make an informed decision, but remember that your attorney will only be able to provide legal support. If what you need is psychological counseling, you can ask for referrals, but your attorney is probably not the proper person to provide such counseling. You will probably have lower costs, and better results, if you use mental health professionals or friends and family as emotional sounding boards.

Determine the level of experience you think you need in your attorney. For example, if you have had a short marriage, with no children, and few assets, an attorney with less experience might be a good value for your legal needs. Many successful firms often also have bright associates who practice at a lower hourly rate, but are supervised by older and more experienced attorneys. By hiring these associates, you get the best of both worlds—divorce expertise from a well-known firm at a reasonable cost. However, if you are anticipating a difficult custody dispute or have complex or substantial assets, a more experienced attorney may better meet your needs.

Consider the qualities in an attorney that are important to you. Even the most experienced and skilled attorney is not right for every person. Ask yourself what you are really looking for in an attorney so you can make your choice with these standards in mind.

As with most things, it is generally easier and far less expensive to get all aspects of your divorce proceeding right the first time than to try to fix errors and omissions after the fact. Finding a competent and knowledgeable attorney at the outset is your best bet to eliminate, to the extent possible, having to face future proceedings after the divorce on the basis of procedural or legal errors.

It is important that you are confident in the attorney you hire. If you are unsure about whether or not the attorney is really listening to you or understanding your concerns, keep looking until you find one who will. Your divorce is an important matter. It's critical that you have a professional you can trust.

3.3   Should I hire a "bulldog"—a very aggressive attorney?

Again, consider the qualities in an attorney that are important to you. A bulldog may promise to be overly aggressive and take your spouse for everything he or she is worth. However, it may be important to you to create a mutually respectful relationship with your spouse during and after the divorce, especially if there are minor children involved.

Additionally, expect the cost of your divorce to exponentially increase if your attorney is unwilling to negotiate and drags your spouse into court at every opportunity. Look for an attorney who can represent you with zealous advocacy, while maintaining a high level of courtesy, professionalism, and integrity.

3.4   Should I interview more than one attorney?

Be willing to interview more than one attorney. Every attorney has different strengths, and it is important that you find the one that is right for you. Sometimes it is only by meeting with more than one attorney that you see clearly who will best be able to help you reach your goals in the way you want.

Because most established attorneys charge for consultations, there can be a significant cost to multiple consultations. But, if possible, you should do whatever is necessary to be comfortable that you are making the right choice. Changing attorneys in the middle of litigation can be stressful and costly. It is wise to invest the energy at the outset to make the right choice.

3.5   My spouse says that because we're still friends we should use the same attorney for the divorce. Is this a good idea?

No. Even the most amicable of divorcing couples usually have differing interests. In most cases, an attorney is ethically prohibited from representing two people with conflicting interests who are in dispute. For this reason, it is never recommended that an attorney represent both parties to a divorce.

Sometimes couples have reached agreements without understanding all of their rights under the law, or even knowing what issues are actually at stake. A person facing divorce will often benefit from receiving further legal advice on complicated matters such as tax considerations, retirement, and health insurance issues. When making such decisions that may affect your financial future, it is important to receive advice from an attorney whose only duty is to protect your interests.

When parties negotiate their own agreement, it is not uncommon for one party to retain an attorney and for the other party not to do so. In such cases, the party with the attorney files the petition for dissolution of marriage, and any agreements reached between the parties are typically written up in a marital settlement agreement and sent to the unrepresented spouse for approval. Oftentimes in New Mexico, if both parties have agreed to the terms of a divorce and have set those terms out clearly in the documents they are filing, there may never be a court hearing. In some New Mexico courts, the judges prefer that the parties appear before the court and confirm in person that they understand the agreements that they have reached and set out in the documents filed with the court.

If your spouse has filed for divorce and said that you do not need an attorney, you should nevertheless meet with an attorney for advice on how proceeding without an attorney could affect your legal rights and to review any paperwork that has been sent to you. Although you may trust your spouse and his/her attorney, know your rights before signing any agreements. Sometimes, the important thing is not what a document says, but what it does not say. While attorneys are trained to look for such issues, most people without legal training are not equipped to do so. A judge will generally not let a person come back to court later to try to change an agreement based upon a lack of knowledge or an unwillingness to consult with their own attorney.

3.6 What can I expect at an initial consultation with an attorney?

The nature of the advice you get from an attorney in an initial consultation will depend upon what stage of the process you are in when you meet. You may be deciding whether you want a divorce, you may be planning for a possible divorce in the future, you may be ready to file for divorce right away, or your spouse may have initiated an action against you.

During the meeting, you will have an opportunity to provide the following information to the attorney:

- A brief history of the marriage
- Background information regarding yourself, your spouse, and your children
- Your immediate situation
- Your intentions and goals regarding your relationship with your spouse
- What information you are seeking from the attorney during the consultation

You can expect the attorney to relay the following information to you:

- The procedure for divorce in New Mexico
- Litigation alternative options such as mediation, collaboration, or settlement facilitation
- An initial review of the issues most important in your case
- A preliminary assessment of your rights and responsibilities under the law
- Background information regarding the firm
- Information about fees, billing, and office procedures

The initial consultation is an opportunity for you to ask all of the questions you have at the time of the meeting. Some questions may be impossible for the attorney to answer at that time because additional information or research is needed.

It is important to remember that no attorney can—or ever should—guarantee you a specific result. There is almost always some doubt as to potential outcomes. The legal process is not perfect or always predictable. Anyone involved can see things differently, or make mistakes, even when it seems to you that the evidence mandates a different result.

3.7 What information should I take with me to the first meeting with my attorney?

Attorneys differ on the amount of information they like to see at an initial consultation. Some attorneys ask you to complete a detailed questionnaire at the time of your first meeting. Ask whether it is possible to do this before the first meeting with the attorney. This can allow you to provide more complete information and to make the most of your appointment time with the attorney.

If a court proceeding of any kind has been initiated by either you or your spouse, it is important to take copies of any court documents with you. If you have ever signed a prenuptial or postnuptial agreement with your spouse, that is another important document for you to bring at the outset of your case.

Also, to organize your thoughts and to provide "your story" to your attorney in a more efficient manner, it is sometimes helpful to prepare a chronology or time line of your relationship. The amount of detail may vary from person to person, but even compiling a list of major dates in your marriage will be helpful to a potential attorney.

If you intend to ask for support, either for yourself or for your children, documents evidencing income of both you and your spouse will also be useful. These might include:

- Recent pay stubs
- Individual and business tax returns, W-2s, and 1099s
- Bank statements showing deposits and withdrawals
- A statement of your monthly budget

At an initial consultation there is usually not enough time for a detailed review of such documents, but if an economic question comes up during the consultation, having such documents on hand may make it possible to give a more complete answer to your question.

If your situation is urgent or you do not have access to the documents mentioned above, do not let that stop you from scheduling your appointment with an attorney. Prompt legal advice about your rights is often more important than having detailed financial information in the beginning. Your attorney can explain to you the options for obtaining these financial records if they are not readily available to you.

3.8 Will the communication with my attorney be confidential?

With few exceptions, attorneys are required to keep confidential all information you provide during the initial consultation and subsequent meetings. This duty of confidentiality also extends to the legal staff working with your attorney, including paralegals and secretaries. The privileged information that you share with your attorney will remain private and confidential, unless such privilege is waived by voluntarily disclosing it to third parties. There are certain rare exceptions. For example, an attorney might be required to reveal information necessary to prevent death or substantial bodily harm. If you have any questions about the scope of the attorney–client privilege, they should be discussed at the beginning of the consultation and before revealing whatever information you have questions about.

3.9 Is there any way that I could waive the attorney–client privilege, as it relates to the duty of confidentiality?

Yes. To ensure that communications between you and your attorney remain confidential, and to protect against the voluntary or involuntary waiver of such privilege, observe the following precautions:

- Refrain from disclosing the content of the communications with your attorney, or discussing in substantive detail the communications with your attorney, to third parties. Such third parties can include friends and family members.
- Social media provides the potential for waiving the attorney–client privilege by publicly disclosing confidential information. Do not post information or send messages relating to your case on Facebook, Twitter, or other social media websites.
- Do not post information relating to your case or communications with your attorney on a personal blog, video blog, online chat rooms, or online message boards.
- Do not use your work-related e-mail to communicate with your attorney, or to discuss your case.

- Depending upon your employer's policy relating to electronic communication, the attorney–client privilege may be waived by communicating with your attorney or by discussing your case through your personal e-mail account (Gmail, Yahoo, etc.) via a company computer. To ensure your communications remain confidential, it is best to communicate only via e-mail from your private e-mail address from your home computer.

3.10 Can I take a friend or family member to my initial consultation?

Yes, but it can raise a complication. Having someone present during your initial consultation can be a source of great support. You might ask the person accompanying you to take notes on your behalf so that you can focus on listening and asking questions. Sometimes, the person you wish to bring has valuable information or specific questions that would be helpful to you in deciding what to do. Remember that this is your consultation, however, and it is important that the attorney hears the facts of your case directly from you.

The complication is that the attorney–client privilege, which recognizes the confidentiality of nearly all communications between you and an attorney, does not extend to a third party present during your consultation. This means that your friend or family member could potentially be called to testify as to what was disclosed during your initial consultation, or otherwise be asked to testify whether you have ever said or admitted something.

Generally, if you are going to disclose information not already known by whomever you wish to bring to a consultation, and you have any concern about that information, you should ask the attorney privately whether it should be discussed with your friend or family member present, before doing so.

3.11 What exactly will my attorney do to help me get a divorce?

Your attorney will play a critical role in helping you get your divorce. You will be actively involved in some of the work, whereas other actions will be taken behind the scenes at the law office, the law library, or the courthouse. Good attorneys will sometimes serve as counselors or sounding boards to help you make good decisions. They will also act as your advocate by asserting your position in negotiations and in court. Finally, attorneys are technicians who draft the legal documents necessary for litigating or resolving your case.

Your attorney may perform any of the following tasks on your behalf:

- Determine which court has jurisdiction to hear your divorce, or any of the issues relating to your divorce.
- Develop a strategy for advising you on all aspects of your divorce, including the nature of your assets and matters concerning your children.
- Prepare legal documents for filing with the court.
- Conduct discovery to obtain information from the other party, which could include depositions, requests for production of documents, requests for admissions, and written interrogatories.
- Appear with you at all court appearances, depositions, and conferences.
- Schedule all deadlines and court appearances.
- Support you in responding to information and discovery requests from your spouse.
- Inform you of actions you are required to take.
- Perform financial analyses of your case, including, when necessary, hiring experts to help find undisclosed assets or money.
- Determine and discuss with you the possibility of utilizing the services of an expert to help address certain aspects of your case.
- Conduct legal research.
- Prepare you for court appearances and depositions.
- Prepare your case for hearings and trial, including preparing exhibits, creating outlines, and interviewing witnesses.
- Advise you regarding your rights under the law and your options as the case progresses.

- Help you prepare a reasonable settlement position and then negotiate on your behalf.
- Counsel you regarding the risks and benefits of negotiated settlement as compared to proceeding to trial.

As your advocate, your attorney is entrusted to take all of the steps necessary to represent you and protect your interests in the divorce.

3.12   What professionals should I expect to work with during my divorce?

Depending upon the issues identified by your attorney, you can expect to work with various types of professionals, such as appraisers, financial professionals, real estate agents, and mental health professionals.

In many courts in New Mexico, if there are issues related to custody or parenting time of minor children, it is mandatory that parents attend mediation to attempt to resolve those issues. The mediator is a neutral third party who has training in mediation and generally in mental health or family systems that will attempt to help you and your spouse negotiate an agreement that is in your children's best interest. The mediator is not a judge and does not make recommendations to the court about custody or time-sharing; however, they may give the parties their opinion based upon their work with children and families. Generally, the parties share the cost of mediation.

When mediation is unsuccessful or where custody or parenting time issues are seriously disputed, the court may appoint a *guardian ad litem (GAL)*. This is an attorney whose duty is to represent the best interest of the child or children in the case. Specific duties of a GAL may be set out by the court or by statute, but they generally have the responsibility to investigate you and your spouse as well as the needs of your child. The GAL may submit reports to the court, or be called as a witness to testify at trial regarding any relevant observations. The fees of a GAL are generally set by the GAL and the court orders the parties to pay those fees either by dividing them equally or by the percentage of income each party has to the other.

Another expert who could be appointed by the court is a psychologist. The role of the psychologist will depend upon the purpose for which she/he was appointed. For example, the psychologist may be appointed to perform a child-custody evaluation, which involves assessing both parents and the child, or this expert may be ordered to evaluate one parent to assess the child's safety while spending time with that parent. Generally a child-custody evaluation involves individual meetings with the psychologist, psychological testing of each party and possibly the child(ren), and consultation with persons close to the child(ren) such as therapists, teachers, and other family members.

In cases that involve complex or unclear financial issues, the court may appoint a forensic financial expert to determine the value of a business, the extent of a community estate, and/or research an allegation of marital waste. This person may also be directed by the court to trace assets to present evidence as to the separate and/or community nature of such asset. Such an expert is typically a CPA or professional business appraiser. The fees for these types of experts are set by the experts themselves and the court generally directs how those fees will be paid.

There are also times where the court will appoint a special master. This person may be appointed to handle a specific procedural issue, such as management of all discovery, or to perform a specific task such as hiring a realtor and attempting to sell a residence or piece of real property. The fees for these services are also generally set by the special master and the court directs the parties on payment of such fees.

3.13 I've been divorced before and I don't think I need an attorney this time; however, my spouse is hiring one. Is it wise to go it alone?

Having gone through a prior divorce, it's likely that you have learned a great deal about the divorce process as well as about your legal rights. However, there are many reasons why you should be extremely cautious about proceeding without legal representation.

It is important to remember that every divorce is different. The length of the marriage, whether or not there are children, the relative financial situation for you and your spouse, the specific assets and debts involved, and your age and health can all affect the financial outcome of your divorce. You may not even know all of the issues presented by your current circumstances.

In addition, the law may have changed since your last divorce. Some aspects of divorce law are likely to change each year. New laws are passed by the New Mexico legislature and new decisions are handed down by the New Mexico Supreme Court and the New Mexico Court of Appeals that affect the rights and responsibilities of people who divorce. Further, there are trends in the law that may be different from when you went through a previous divorce.

In some cases, the involvement of your attorney may be minimal. However, at a minimum, have an initial consultation with an attorney to discuss your rights and have an attorney review any final agreements. You need to understand the extent of your rights and potential obligations, and to be sure you know all of the issues present. The law also allows limited-scope representation, which allows an attorney to perform certain limited services for you rather than formally appearing as your attorney for all phases of a case.

Making informed decisions is critical to obtaining, at the very least, a tolerable outcome in your divorce proceeding. Having competent professional advice is often critical to minimize the chance of an unpleasant surprise during or after divorce as to an issue or choice that was overlooked or mistaken during the divorce process. Some things, once they go wrong, cannot be fixed.

3.14　Can I take my children to meetings with my attorney?

It is best to make other arrangements for your children when you meet with your attorney. Your attorney will be giving you a great deal of important information during your conferences, and it will benefit you to give your full attention.

It is also recommended that you take every measure to keep information about the legal aspects of your divorce away from your children. For example, do not leave court documents in plain sight in your house and do not speak with your attorney or others about the divorce within hearing distance of your children. Not only can knowledge that you are seeing an attorney add to your child's anxiety about the process, it can also make your child a target for questioning by the other parent and can lead to issues with the court. Your standard procedure should be to leave your children out of the divorce process as much as possible.

Most law offices are not designed to accommodate young children and are ordinarily not "childproof." For both your child's well-being and your own peace of mind, explore options for someone to care for your child when you have meetings with your attorney. Also, most courts do not allow minor children to be present at the courthouse for any court hearings or trials and they should not be brought to such proceedings unless specifically directed to do so by the court.

3.15 What is the role of the *paralegal* or *legal assistant* in my attorney's office?

A *paralegal,* or *legal assistant,* is a trained legal professional whose duties include providing support for both you and your attorney. The exact roles paralegals serve vary from office to office, but generally they help with gathering information, reviewing documents with you, providing you updates on your case, informing you of important dates and deadlines, and preparing documents for your attorney to review.

Paralegals can also often answer your questions about the divorce process and developments in your case that do not call for legal advice; these are essentially the "who, what, where, and when" questions that come up in nearly every case. The "why" questions are generally left to your attorney. This is because a paralegal is prohibited by ethical codes and court rules from giving legal advice.

It is important that you respect the limits of the role of the paralegal. Do not get frustrated or angry if a paralegal is unable to answer your questions because they call for a legal opinion; if you get such a response, it means that the paralegal is doing their job correctly. However, a paralegal can answer many questions and provide a great deal of information to you throughout your divorce.

Working with a paralegal can make your divorce easier because he or she is likely to be more available to help you than your attorney who has to attend to other client meetings, settlement conferences, and court proceedings. Working with and communicating with a paralegal can also help manage your legal costs, as the hourly rate for paralegal services is generally less than the rate for attorneys.

3.16   My attorney is not returning my phone calls. What can I do?

You have a right to expect your phone calls, e-mails, and other communications to be responded to by your attorney in a timely fashion. Here are some options to consider:

- Make sure that your messages are being received and have not been lost, misdirected, or sent to "spam."
- Ask to speak to the paralegal or another attorney in the office.
- Send an e-mail or fax telling your attorney that you have been trying to reach him or her by phone and explaining the reason it is important that you receive a call.
- Ask the receptionist to schedule a phone conference for you to speak with your attorney at a specific date and time.
- Schedule a meeting with your attorney to discuss both the issue needing attention as well as your concerns about the communication.

Generally, your attorney wants to provide you with good service. Communication is one of the first rules of professional conduct governing attorney behavior. However, it is also important to remember that you are probably not your attorney's only client, and sometimes attorneys are required by other cases to be in court or in conferences that make them temporarily unavailable to you. There may be a delay in returning calls if the attorney is involved in a complicated or multiday trial or deposition proceedings.

Also, sometimes, if met with multiple demands from many cases at the same time, a law firm has to decide what issues are a priority and may be addressing an emergency situation for another client. Although that can be frustrating, it is helpful to understand that the firm would do the same if it were your emergency. A legal assistant or paralegal should be able to advise you about what is causing the delay in having your call returned and help you come up with a solution for being able to communicate with your attorney.

At your initial consultation, it is a good idea to discuss your attorney's protocol for returning calls and messages. Many offices have a policy of returning all calls or messages within one or two business days; others have different policies. In some offices, a paralegal will return the calls if the attorney is not available. Some offices send regular status reports whether or not anything notable is happening in a case; others do not. Knowing the rules that apply in your attorney's office can reduce frustration on both sides. Also remember that attorneys and their staff are people, too, with illnesses, injuries, emergencies, vacations, and holidays. The key is to be reasonable and to temper your expectations as within the rules of communication you and your attorney agree to follow.

3.17 How do I know when it's time to change attorneys?

Changing attorneys is costly and sometimes can harm your case. Thus, it is not a step to take lightly. You will spend time giving much of the same information to your new attorney that you gave to the one you have discharged. You will incur legal fees for your new attorney to review information that is already familiar to your current attorney. A change in attorneys also may result in a delay in the divorce in order to allow your new attorney to become familiar with all that has occurred in your case.

The following are questions to ask yourself when you're deciding whether to stay with your attorney or to seek new counsel:

- Have I spoken directly to my attorney about my concerns?
- When I expressed concerns, did my attorney take action accordingly?
- Is my attorney open and receptive to what I have to say?
- Am I blaming my attorney for the bad behavior of my spouse or opposing counsel?

- Have I provided my attorney with the information needed for taking the next action?
- Does my attorney have control over the concerns I have, or are my concerns regarding the law on a given subject?
- Would the matters that concern me about my attorney exist no matter who my attorney was?
- Are my concerns the result of a judge's unpredictable actions?
- Is my attorney keeping promises for completing action on my case?
- Do I trust my attorney?
- What would be the advantages of changing attorneys when compared to the cost?
- Is there something that a new attorney could do in my case that my current attorney cannot do?
- Do I believe my attorney will support me to achieve the outcome I'm seeking in my divorce?

Every effort should be made to resolve concerns with your attorney prior to changing attorneys. In addition, if you are considering changing attorneys, it is a good idea to set an appointment with your current attorney to review your specific concerns and see if there is a way to resolve them. You may also want to schedule a second-opinion consultation with another attorney to see if they have a different perspective on your case.

In the event your current attorney does not or cannot resolve your concerns to your satisfaction and you think your case may be better handled by another attorney, it may be time to switch attorneys.

3.18 Are there certain expectations that I should have when working with my legal team?

Yes. Your legal team should be able to provide you with support and guidance during your divorce process. There are certain actions you can expect your legal team to do for you during your divorce:

- Discuss with you the ramifications of filing a court action and advise you on the actions you should take first. There may be important steps to take before you initiate the legal process. Your legal team can support you to be well prepared prior to initiating divorce.

- Take action to obtain a temporary court order or to enforce existing orders. Temporary court orders are often needed to ensure clarity regarding your rights and responsibilities while your divorce is pending. Currently in New Mexico, there is a standard temporary order issued in every divorce or family action called a *temporary domestic order (TDO)*. You should be familiar with the contents of the TDO prior to filing any action. Your legal team can help you become familiar with the TDO and obtain other temporary orders and ask the court to enforce these orders if there is a violation.

- Explain the legal process during each step of your case. Understanding the legal process reduces the stress of your divorce. Your legal team can guide you every step of the way.

- Listen to your concerns and answer your questions. Although only attorneys can give you legal advice, everyone on your team is available to listen, to provide support, and to direct you to the right person to help.

- Support you in developing your parenting plan. Many parents do not know how to decide what type of parenting plan is best for their children. Your legal team can help you look at the needs of your children and offer advice based on their experience in working with families.

- Support you in the completion of your discovery responses and preparation for depositions. The discovery process can be overwhelming for anyone. You will be asked to provide detailed information and many documents. Your legal team can make this job easier. If your case involves depositions, your legal team will support you to be fully prepared for the experience.

- Identify important issues, analyze the evidence, and advise you accordingly. Divorce is complex. Often there is a great deal of uncertainty. Your legal team can analyze the unique facts of your case and advise you based upon the law and their expertise.

- Communicate with the opposing party's attorney to try to resolve issues without going to court, and to keep your case progressing. Although your attorney cannot control the actions of the opposing party or their attorney, your attorney can initiate communication with the other attorney as your advocate. Telephoning, e-mailing, or writing to opposing counsel are actions your legal team can take to encourage cooperation and to keep your divorce moving forward at the pace you want without the expense of contested litigation.

- Think creatively regarding challenges with your case and provide options for your consideration. At the outset, you may see many obstacles to reaching a final resolution. Your legal team can offer creative ideas for resolving challenges and help you to explore your options to achieve the best possible outcome.

- Facilitate the settlement process. Although your legal team can never make the other party settle, your attorney can take actions to promote settlement. They can prepare settlement proposals, invite settlement conferences, and negotiate zealously on your behalf.

3.19 Are there certain things my attorney will not be able to do?

Yes. Although there are many ways in which your attorney can support you during your divorce, there are also things your attorney will not be able to accomplish, including the following:

- Force the other parent to exercise their parenting time. Your attorney cannot force a parent to exercise parenting time. However, be mindful that a chronic neglect of parenting time may be a basis for modifying your parenting plan. Tell your attorney if the other parent is repeatedly failing to exercise their parenting time.

- Force the other party to respond to a settlement proposal. Your attorney may send proposals or make requests to opposing counsel; however, there is no duty for the other attorney to respond. After repeated follow-ups without a response, it may be clear that no response is coming. At that time, your attorney will decide whether the issues merit court action. Both parties must agree on all terms for a case to be settled without a trial. If one party wants to proceed to trial, even over a single issue, he/she will be able to do so.

- Control the tone of communication from opposing counsel or communications from the other party, or the other party's family members. Unfortunately, communication from the opposing attorney may sometimes appear rude, condescending, or demanding. Your legal team cannot stop an attorney from using these tactics. Absent a pattern of harassment, your attorney cannot stop the other party or third parties from contacting you. If you do not want the contact, talk with your attorney about how to best handle the situation. Of course, appropriate communication regarding your children is always encouraged.

- Ask the court to compensate you for every wrong done to you by the other party over the course of your marriage. Although your attorney will empathize with valid complaints, the law cannot provide justice or compensation for everything that occurred during a marriage. The attorney will focus on the most important issues and the ones that will yield the best outcome in the end. Raising numerous small issues may distract from your most important goals.

- Remedy poor financial decisions made during the marriage. With few exceptions, the court's duty is to divide the marital estate as it currently exists. The judge will not attempt to remedy all past financial wrongs, such as overspending or poor investments by your spouse.

- Control how the other party parents your children during his/her parenting time. Each parent has strengths and weaknesses. Absent serious misconduct or the special needs of a child, most judges will not issue orders regarding bedtimes, amount of TV watching or video game playing, discipline methods, clothing, or diet. Of course, any suspected abuse should be reported immediately to the appropriate authorities.

- Demand an accounting of how a parent uses court-ordered child support. Absent extraordinary circumstances, the court will not order the other parent to provide an accounting for the use of child support.

- Leverage money for rights regarding your children. Tactics oriented toward asserting custody rights as leverage toward attaining financial goals will be discouraged. Your attorney should negotiate parenting issues based solely on considerations related to your child, then separately negotiate child support based on financial considerations.

- Guarantee payment of child support and alimony. Enforcement of payment of support is only possible when it is court-ordered. However, even with a court order, you may experience inconsistent timing of payments due to job loss or refusal to pay. Talk with your attorney if a pattern of repeated missed payments has developed.

- Collect child care and uninsured medical expenses if provisions of the final decree of dissolution of marriage are not complied with. If your final decree of dissolution of marriage requires you to provide documentation of payment of expenses to the other party and you fail to do so, you could be prohibited from collecting reimbursement for those expenses. Follow the court's orders regarding providing documentation to the other parent, even if they do not pay as they should. Always keep records of expenses and payments made by each parent, and keep copies of communications with the other parent regarding payment/reimbursement. It is much easier to keep these records on an ongoing basis than to get copies of old checks, day care bills, medical bills, and insurance documents at a later time.

4

Attorney Fees and Costs

Any time you make a major investment, you want to know what the cost is going to be and what you are getting for your money. Investing in quality legal representation for your divorce is no different.

The cost of your divorce might be one of your greatest concerns. Because of this, you will want to be an intelligent consumer of legal services. You want quality, but you also want to get the best value for the fees you are paying.

Legal fees for a divorce can be costly and the total expense is not always predictable. With that said, there are many actions you can take to control and estimate the cost, including the following:

- Develop a plan early on for how you will finance your divorce.
- Speak openly with your attorney about fees from the outset.
- Learn as much as you can about how you will be charged.
- Insist on a written fee agreement.

By being informed, aware, and wise, your financial investment in your divorce will be money well spent to protect your future.

4.1   Can I get free legal advice from an attorney over the phone?

Every law firm has its own policy regarding attorneys talking to people who are not yet clients of the firm. Most questions about your divorce are too complex for an attorney to give a meaningful answer during a brief phone call.

Getting reliable and specific answers to questions you have about your divorce requires a complete look at the facts, circumstances, and background of your marriage. To obtain good legal advice, it's best to schedule an initial consultation with an attorney who handles divorces.

4.2   Will I be charged for an initial consultation with an attorney?

It depends. Some attorneys give free consultations, whereas others charge a fee. When scheduling your appointment, you should be told the amount of the fee in advance. Payment is ordinarily due at the time of the consultation.

4.3   If I decide to hire an attorney, when do I have to pay him or her?

If your attorney charges for an initial consultation, be prepared to make payment at the time of your meeting. At the close of your consultation, the attorney may tell you the amount of the retainer needed by the law firm to handle your divorce. However, you are not expected to pay the retainer at the time of your first meeting. Rather, the retainer is paid after the attorney has accepted your case, you have decided to hire the attorney, and you are ready to proceed.

4.4   What exactly is a *retainer* and how much will mine be?

A *retainer* is a deposit paid to your attorney in advance for services to be performed and costs to be incurred in your divorce. This will be either an amount paid toward a "flat fee" for your divorce, or (much more commonly) an advance deposit for services that will be charged by the hour.

If your case is accepted by the law firm, expect the attorney to request a retainer before work begins on your case. The amount of the retainer may vary from hundreds of dollars to several thousand dollars, depending upon the nature of your case. Divorces involving contested custody, businesses, or interstate disputes, for example, are all likely to require higher retainers.

Probably the most important question in terms of how much a case will cost is just how much the parties to the case are determined to fight about whatever issues exist in the case, rather than working together to solve them. The more contested a case appears to be, the higher the retainer will usually be. Other factors that can affect the amount of the retainer include the nature and number of disputed issues.

4.5 Will my attorney accept my divorce case on a *contingency-fee* basis?

No. A *contingency fee* is one in which the attorney agrees to do work in exchange for a fixed percentage of the recovery obtained. In New Mexico, attorneys are prohibited from entering into a contingent-fee contract in any divorce case. Your attorney may not accept payment based upon securing your divorce, the amount of alimony or support awarded, or the division of the property settlement.

4.6 How much does it cost to get a divorce?

The cost of your divorce will depend upon many factors. Some attorneys perform divorces for a flat fee, but most charge by the hour. A flat fee is a fixed amount for the legal services being provided. A flat fee is more likely to be used when there are no children of the marriage and the parties have agreed upon the division of their property and debts. Most New Mexico attorneys charge by the hour for divorces because it is usually difficult to tell how much time and effort will be required to complete the case.

It is important that your discussion of the cost of your divorce begin at your first meeting with your attorney. It is customary for family law attorneys to request a retainer, also known as a *fee advance,* prior to beginning work on your case. In planning for paying an attorney, take into consideration replenishment of the retainer as funds are used in your case.

Be sure to ask your attorney what portion, if any, of the retainer is refundable if the case is finished quickly, if you choose not to continue with the case, or if you terminate your relationship with the attorney.

4.7 What are typical hourly rates for a divorce attorney?

In New Mexico, attorneys who practice in the divorce area charge anywhere from $150 to $500 per hour. The rate your attorney charges may depend upon factors such as skill, reputation, experience, exclusive focus on divorce law, and what other attorneys in the area are charging.

It is common for more experienced attorneys in a firm to have a higher hourly rate than more junior attorneys in the firm, who are usually called *associates.* If you have a concern about being able to pay an attorney's hourly rate, but you would like to hire that attorney's firm, consider asking to work with an associate attorney in the firm who is likely to charge a lower hourly rate. Associates are often supervised and trained by the senior partners, and are fully capable of handling your case.

4.8 If I can't afford to pay the full amount of the retainer, can I make monthly payments to my attorney?

Every law firm has its own policies regarding payment arrangements for divorce clients. Sometimes these arrangements are tailored to the specific client, but most law firms have policies of some sort as to how they handle such requests.

Most attorneys will require a substantial retainer to be paid at the outset of your case. Some attorneys may accept monthly payments in lieu of the retainer or take a very small retainer followed by monthly payments. Others may require additional retainers as your case progresses. Ask frank questions of your attorney to have clarity about your responsibility for payment of legal fees.

4.9 I agreed to pay my attorney a substantial retainer to begin my case. Will I still have to make monthly payments?

Ask your attorney what will be expected of you regarding payments on your account while the divorce is in progress. Be clear on whether monthly payments on your account will be expected, whether it is likely that you will be asked to pay additional retainers, and whether the firm charges interest on past-due accounts. Regular payments to your attorney can help you avoid having a tremendously burdensome legal bill at the end of your case. Additionally, you may also be required to keep a minimum credit balance on your account to ensure your case is adequately funded for ongoing work by your legal team. Your written retainer agreement should clearly detail all of these provisions.

4.10 I've been turned down by programs providing free legal services. How can I get the money to pay for an attorney?

There are a number of options to consider when it seems as though you are without funds to pay an attorney.

First, ask yourself whether or not you have closely examined all sources of funds readily available to you. Sometimes, people simply overlook money that they might be able to access. Consider taking out a loan or charging your retainer on a credit card.

Next, talk to your family members and friends. Often, those close to you are concerned about your future and would be willing to support you in your goal of having your rights protected. If the retainer is too much money to request from a single individual, consider whether several persons might each be able to contribute a lesser amount to help you hire an attorney.

If your case is not urgent, consider developing a plan for saving the money you need to proceed with a divorce. Your attorney may be willing to receive and hold monthly payments until you have paid an amount sufficient to pay the initial retainer.

Under certain circumstances, an attorney might be willing to be paid from the proceeds of a property settlement. If you and your spouse have acquired substantial assets during the marriage, you may be able to find an attorney who will wait to be paid until the assets are divided at the conclusion of the divorce. Finding such an attorney may be difficult as most require that their services are paid for at the time they are provided.

4.11 My attorney gave me an estimate of the cost of my divorce and it sounds reasonable. Do I still need a written fee agreement?

Yes. Insist upon a written agreement with your attorney. This is essential not only to define the scope of the services for which you have hired your attorney, but also to ensure that you have clarity about matters such as your attorney's hourly rate, whether you will be billed for certain costs such as copying, and when you can expect to receive statements on your account.

A clear fee agreement reduces the risk of misunderstandings between you and your attorney. It supports you both in being clear about your promises to each other so that your focus can be on the legal services being provided rather than on disputes about your fees.

4.12 How will I know how the fees and charges are accumulating?

Be sure your written fee agreement with your attorney is completely clear about how you will be informed about the status of your account. If your attorney agrees to handle your divorce for a flat fee, your fee agreement should clearly set forth what is included in the fee. Most attorneys charge by the hour for handling divorces.

At the outset of your case, be sure your written fee agreement includes a provision for the attorney to provide you with regular statements of your account. It is reasonable to ask that these be provided monthly.

Review the statement of your account promptly after you receive it. Check to make sure there are no errors, such as duplicate billing entries. If your statement reflects work that you were unaware was performed, call for clarification. Your attorney's office should welcome any questions you have about services it is providing, and why.

Your statement might also include filing fees, court reporter fees for transcripts of court testimony or depositions, copy expenses, or interest charged on your account. If several weeks have passed and you have not received a statement on your account, call your attorney's office to request one. Legal fees can mount quickly, and it is important that you stay aware of the status of your legal expenses.

4.13 What other expenses are related to the divorce litigation besides attorney fees?

Talk to your attorney about costs other than the attorney fees. Ask whether it is likely there will be filing fees, court reporter expenses, subpoenas, expert-witness fees, mediation, or parenting class fees. Expert-witness fees can be a substantial expense, ranging from hundreds to thousands of dollars, depending upon the type of expert and the extent to which he or she is involved in your case.

Speak frankly with your attorney about these costs so that together you can make the best decisions about how to use your budget for the litigation.

4.14 Who pays for the experts such as accountants, appraisers, psychologists, guardians *ad litem,* and settlement facilitators?

Costs for the services of experts, whether appointed by the court or hired by the parties, are ordinarily paid for by the parties.

The judge can order these fees to be shared equally by the parties or paid in proportion to the parties' respective incomes. Depending upon the circumstances, one party can be ordered to pay the entire fee which can sometimes be reapportioned at the conclusion of the case.

In New Mexico, guardians *ad litem* must be attorneys and it is common for them to have similar billing practices to divorce attorneys. It is typical for guardians *ad litem* to request a retainer and charge an hourly rate for their services.

Psychologists either charge by the hour or set a flat fee depending on what they are called upon to do. Again, the court can order one party to pay this fee or both parties to share in the expense. It is not uncommon for a psychologist to request payment in advance and hold the release of an expert report until fees are paid.

Settlement facilitators either charge a flat fee per session or an hourly rate fee. Generally the settlement facilitator's fees will be equally shared or paid in proportion to the parties' incomes. In most instances the settlement facilitator will require payment prior to the settlement facilitation.

The fees for many experts, including accountants and appraisers, will vary depending upon whether the individuals are called upon to provide only a specific service such as a business valuation or an appraisal, or whether they will need to prepare for giving testimony and appear as a witness at trial.

Talk to your attorney about these costs so you are aware of what to expect.

4.15   What factors will impact the cost of my divorce?

Although it is difficult to predict how much your legal fees will be, the following are some of the factors that affect the cost:

- Whether there are children
- Whether child custody is agreed upon by the parties
- Whether there are novel legal questions
- Whether a pension plan will be divided between the parties
- The nature of the issues contested and the evidence required to prove them
- The number of issues agreed to by the parties
- The cooperation of the opposing party and opposing counsel
- Whether there are additional costs, such as fees for expert witnesses, guardians *ad litem,* or a settlement facilitator
- The frequency of your communication with your legal team
- The ability of the parties to communicate with each other, as well as the client's ability to communicate with his/her attorney
- The promptness with which information is provided and/or exchanged between both the clients and the attorneys
- The hourly rate of the attorney
- The time it will take to conclude your divorce

Communicating with your attorney regularly about your legal fees will help you to have a better understanding of the overall cost as your case proceeds.

4.16   Will my attorney charge for phone calls and e-mails?

Unless your case is being handled on a flat-fee basis, you should expect to be billed for any communication with your attorney or their staff. Many of the professional services provided by attorneys are done by phone and by e-mail. This time can be spent giving legal advice, negotiation, or gathering information to protect your interests. These calls and e-mails are all legal services for which you should anticipate being charged by your attorney.

To make the most of your time during attorney phone calls, plan your call in advance. Organize the information you want to relay, your questions, and any concerns to be addressed. Write a checklist if that is helpful to you in staying organized. Being clear and focused during each phone call will help ensure that your fees are well spent.

The same is true for e-mail correspondence that you intend to send to your attorney. Don't send a string of one-question e-mails when you can include all of your questions in one e-mail. Try to be as organized and to the point as possible. This will save you considerable money in the long run.

4.17   Will I be charged for talking to the staff at my attorney's office?

Usually, yes. Check the terms of your fee agreement with your attorney. Whether you are charged fees for talking to non-attorney members of the law office may depend upon their role in the office. For example, many law firms charge for the services of paralegals and law clerks.

Remember that non-attorneys cannot give legal advice. Don't expect the receptionist or a paralegal to give you an opinion regarding whether you will win custody or receive alimony.

Your attorney's support staff will be able relay your messages and receive information from you. They may also be able to answer many of your questions, especially those questions that are procedural rather than substantive. For example, a paralegal assigned to a case should know when hearings are calendared, or whether filings have been made in a case. Allowing this type of support from within the firm is an important way to control your legal fees.

4.18   What is a *trial retainer* and will I have to pay one?

A *trial retainer* is different from a regular retainer, which was discussed earlier in this chapter. A trial retainer is a sum of money paid on your account with your attorney when it appears as though your case may not settle and will likely proceed to trial. The purpose of the trial retainer is to fund the work needed to prepare for trial and for the services provided the day(s) of trial.

Confirm with your attorney that any unearned portion of your trial retainer will be refunded if your case settles, or if the trial costs prove to be less expensive than anticipated. Ask your attorney in advance whether and when a trial retainer might be required in your case so that you can avoid surprises and plan your budget accordingly.

4.19   How do I know whether I should spend the money my attorney says it will require to take my case to trial?

Deciding whether to take a case to trial or to settle is often the most challenging point in the divorce process. This decision should be made with the support of your attorney.

When the issues in dispute are primarily financial, often the decision about settlement is related to the costs of going to trial. Your attorney might refer to this as a *cost/benefit analysis*. Be clear about just how far apart you and your spouse are on the financial matters and compare this to the estimated costs of going to trial. You also need to gain some sense of the likelihood of winning on each issue in contest. By comparing these amounts, you can decide whether reaching a compromise and having certainty about the outcome would be better than paying legal fees and not knowing how your case will be resolved by the judge.

4.20 If someone other than me pays my legal fees, will my attorney give that person private information about my divorce?

If someone other than you is paying your legal bills, your attorney still has an ethical duty to maintain confidentiality. Without your permission, your attorney should not disclose information to others about your case.

Your attorney can only communicate with your family members with your permission. Expect to be charged by your attorney for the time spent on these calls or meetings. Regardless of the opinions of the person who pays your attorney fees, your attorney's duty is to remain your advocate.

4.21 Can I ask the court to order my spouse to pay my attorney's fees?

Yes. If you want to ask the court to order your spouse to pay any portion of your legal fees, be sure to discuss this with your attorney at the first opportunity. Most attorneys will treat the obligation for your legal fees as yours until the other party has made payment. If your case is likely to require costly experts and your spouse has a much greater ability to pay these expenses than you do, talk to your attorney about the possibility of filing a motion with the court asking your spouse to advance these costs while the case is pending.

4.22 What happens if I don't pay my attorney the fees I promised to pay?

The ethical rules for attorneys allow your attorney to withdraw from your case if you do not comply with your fee agreement. Consequently, it is important that you keep the promises you have made regarding your account.

If you are having difficulty paying your attorney's fees, talk with your attorney about payment options. Consider borrowing the funds, using your credit card, or asking for help from friends and family.

Above all, do not avoid communication with your attorney if you are having challenges making payment. Keeping in touch with your attorney is essential in order for you to have an advocate at all stages of your divorce.

4.23   Is there any way I can reduce some of the expenses of getting a divorce?

Litigation of any kind can be expensive, and divorces are no exception. The good news is that there are many ways that you can help control the expense, including the following:

- *Put it in writing.* If you need to relay information that is important but not urgent, consider providing it to your attorney by e-mail, fax, or regular mail. This creates a prompt and accurate record for your file and usually takes less time than exchanging phone messages and talking on the phone.

- *Keep your attorney informed.* Just as your attorney should keep you up-to-date on the status of your case, you need to do the same. Keep your attorney advised about any major developments in your life such as plans to move, plans to have someone move into your home, a change in your employment status, or your desire to buy or sell a property. During your divorce, your address, phone number, or e-mail address may change. Be sure to notify your attorney immediately of any changes to your contact information. Your attorney may need to reach you with information, and reaching you in a timely manner may help avoid more costly fees later.

- *Obtain copies of documents.* An important part of litigation includes reviewing documents such as tax returns, account statements, report cards, or medical records. Your attorney will ordinarily be able to request, or *subpoena,* these items, but many may be readily available to you directly upon request.

- *Consult your attorney's website.* If your attorney has a website, it may be a great source of useful information. The answers to commonly asked questions about the divorce process can often be found there.

- *Utilize support professionals.* Get to know the support staff at your attorney's office. The receptionist, paralegal, legal secretary, or law clerk may have the answer to your question. Although only attorneys are able to give you legal advice, other support professionals can often answer your questions regarding the status of your case. These professionals can also relay information from your attorney to you at a much lower cost than you speaking directly to the attorney. Just as your communication with your attorney, all communication with any professionals in a law firm is required to be kept strictly confidential.

- *Consider working with an associate attorney.* Although the senior attorneys or partners in a law firm may have more experience, you may find that working with an associate attorney on some or all tasks is a good option. Hourly rates for an associate attorney are typically lower than those charged by a senior partner. Frequently, the associate attorney has trained under a senior partner and developed excellent skills and knowledge of the law. Many associate attorneys are also very experienced.

  Discuss with the firm the benefits of working with a senior or an associate attorney in light of the nature of your case, the expertise of the respective attorneys, and the potential cost savings to you

  Some firms work as a team and you may find multiple attorneys or staff members are working on your case. This is usually done to maximize the usefulness to you of the expertise of the firm's staff and to keep costs down for you, by having tasks performed as efficiently as possible. If you think this method might work well in your case, talk frankly with your attorney or with the firm's administrator.

- *Leave detailed messages.* If your attorney knows the information you are seeking, she or he can often get the answer to you before they are able to return your call. This not only gets your answer faster, but also reduces costs.

- *Discuss more than one matter during a call.* It is not unusual for clients to have many questions during litigation. If your question is not urgent, consider waiting to call until you have more than one inquiry. However, never hesitate to call to ask any necessary legal questions.

- *Provide timely responses to requests for information.* Whenever possible, provide information requested by your attorney in a timely manner. This avoids the cost of follow-up requests or actions by your attorney and the additional expense of extending the time in litigation.
- *Carefully review your monthly statements.* Scrutinize your monthly billing statements closely. If you believe an error has been made, contact your attorney's office right away to discuss your concerns.
- *Remain open to settlement.* Be aware of when your disagreement with your spouse is about smaller sums of money than the cost of taking the issue to court to be resolved.

4.24 I don't have any money and I need a divorce. What are my options?

New Mexico Domestic Relations forms are available online at www.nmcourts.gov. You may consider sitting down with your spouse and attempting to resolve your issues in dispute so that these forms can be filled out without the need for an attorney. These forms are very basic and may not provide for every issue in your case. If you wish to have additional peace of mind, many attorneys are willing to review these documents at his/her hourly rate.

At present, there is a divorce workshop each month organized by the State Bar of New Mexico Family Law Section, along with the Albuquerque Bar Association and the New Mexico Collaborative Practice Group. This workshop is held on the first Wednesday of each month from 6:00 P.M. to 8:00 P.M. at the State Bar of New Mexico and is geared toward informing the community about their options and the steps necessary to get a divorce in New Mexico.

For more information on how to obtain a no-cost or low-cost divorce you can contact one of the following organizations (*see* Resources for contact information):

- The Second Judicial District Center for Self Help and Dispute Resolution
- New Mexico Legal Aid

- The State Bar of New Mexico General Referral Program
- Law Access New Mexico
- The University of New Mexico School of Law Clinical Program

Many of these organizations provide guidance rather than legal representation. The organizations that provide actual representation have a screening process for potential clients, as well as limits on the nature of the cases they take. The demand for their services is also usually greater than the number of attorneys available to handle cases. Consequently, if you are eligible for legal services from one of these programs, you should anticipate being on a waiting list. In short, if you have very little income and few assets, you are likely to experience some delay in obtaining an attorney. If you believe you might be eligible for participation in one of these programs, inquire early to increase your opportunity to get the legal help you are seeking.

4.25 I don't have much money, but I need to get a divorce as quickly as possible. What should I do?

If you have some money and want to divorce as soon as possible, consider some of these options:

- Borrow the legal fees from friends or family. Often those close to you are concerned about your future and would be pleased to support you in your goal of having your rights protected. Although this may be uncomfortable, remember that most people will appreciate that you trusted them enough to ask for their help. If the retainer is too much money to request from a single individual, consider whether a handful of persons might each be able to contribute a lesser amount to help you reach your goal of hiring an attorney.
- Charge the legal fees on a low-interest credit card or consider taking out a loan.
- Start saving. If your case is not urgent, consider developing a plan for saving the money you need to proceed with a divorce. Your attorney may be willing

to receive and hold monthly payments until you have paid an amount sufficient to pay the initial retainer.

- Talk to your attorney about using money held in a joint account with your spouse.

- Find an attorney who will work with you on a monthly payment basis.

- Ask your attorney about your spouse paying for your legal fees.

- Ask your attorney about being paid from the proceeds of the property settlement. If you and your spouse have acquired substantial assets during the marriage, you may be able to find an attorney who will wait to be paid until the assets are divided at the conclusion of the divorce.

Closely examine all sources of funds readily available to you, as you may have overlooked money that might be easily accessible to you.

Contact the State Bar of New Mexico General Referral Program at (505) 797-6066 or (800) 876-6227. Let them know you have some ability to pay and ask for help finding an attorney who will take your case for a reduced fee.

Even if you do not have the financial resources to proceed with your divorce at this time, consult with an attorney to learn your rights and to develop an action plan for steps you can take between now and the time you are able to proceed. Often there are measures you can take right away to protect yourself until you have the money to proceed with your divorce.

4.26 Is there anything I can do on my own to get support for my children if I don't have money for an attorney for a divorce?

Yes. If you need support for your children, contact the New Mexico Child Support Enforcement Division (CSED) for help in obtaining a child-support order. Although they cannot help you with matters such as custody or property division, they can pursue support from your spouse for your children.

Call toll free at (800) 288-7207 from within New Mexico or (800) 585-7631 toll free from outside New Mexico, or visit their website at: www.hsd.state.nm.us/LookingForAssistance/ Child_Support.aspx.

5

The Discovery Process

Discovery is one of the least talked about steps in divorce, but it is often among the most important. *Discovery* is the pretrial phase in a lawsuit during which each party can obtain evidence from the opposing party. The purpose of discovery is to ensure that both you and your spouse have access to all relevant information. In this way, you can either negotiate a fair agreement or have all of the facts and documents to present to the judge at trial. The discovery process enables you and your spouse to meet on a more level playing field when it comes to settling your case or taking it to trial. You and your spouse both need the same information if you hope to reach agreement on any of the issues in your divorce. Similarly, a judge must know all of the facts to make a fair decision.

The discovery process may seem tedious at times because of the need to obtain and provide lots of detailed information. Completing it, however, can give tremendous clarity about the issues in your divorce. Trust your attorney's advice about the importance of having the necessary evidence as you complete the discovery process in order to reach your goals in your divorce.

5.1 What types of discovery might be done by my attorney or my spouse's attorney?

Types of discovery include:

- *Interrogatories*—written questions that must be answered under oath

- *Requests for production of documents*—requests that certain documents be provided by you or your spouse
- *Requests for admissions*—requests that certain facts be admitted or denied
- *Subpoena of documents*—requests that a third party, an individual or corporation, provide certain documents
- *Depositions*—questions asked and answered under oath in the presence of a court reporter but outside the presence of a judge

Factors that can influence the type of discovery conducted in your divorce can include:

- The types of issues in dispute
- How much access you and your spouse have to needed information
- The level of cooperation in sharing information
- The budget available for performing discovery

Talk to your attorney about the nature and extent of discovery anticipated in your case.

5.2   How long does the discovery process take?

Discovery can take anywhere from a few weeks to a number of months, depending upon factors such as the complexity of the case, the cooperation of you and your spouse, and whether expert witnesses are involved.

The New Mexico Rules of Discovery provide that interrogatories, requests for production of documents, and requests for admissions be responded to within thirty days.

5.3   My attorney insists that we conduct discovery, but I don't want to spend the time and money on it. Is it really necessary?

The discovery process can be critical to a successful outcome in your case for several reasons:

- It increases the likelihood that any agreements reached are based on accurate information.
- It provides necessary information for deciding whether to settle or proceed to trial.

- It supports the preparation of defenses by providing information regarding your spouse's case.
- It avoids surprises at trial, such as unexpected witness testimony.
- It ensures all potential issues are identified by your attorney.

Discuss with your attorney the intention behind the discovery being conducted in your case to ensure it is consistent with your goals and is a meaningful investment of your legal fees.

5.4   I just received interrogatories and request for production from my spouse's attorney. My attorney wants me to respond within two weeks. I'll never make the deadline. What can I do?

Answering your discovery promptly will help move your case forward and help control your legal fees. There are steps you can take to make this task easier. First, look at all of the questions. Many of them will not apply or your answers will be a simple "yes" or "no."

- Ask a friend to help you. It is important that you develop the practice of letting others help you while you are going through your divorce. Chances are that you will make great progress in just a couple of hours with a friend helping you.
- Break it down into smaller tasks. If you answer just a few questions a day, the job will not be so overwhelming.
- Call your attorney. Ask whether a paralegal in the office can help you organize the needed information or determine whether some of it can be provided at a later date.

Delays in the discovery process often lead to frustration by clients and attorneys. Do your best to provide the information in a timely manner with the help of others.

5.5   I don't have access to my documents and my spouse is being uncooperative in providing my attorney with information. Can my attorney request information directly from an employer or financial institution?

Yes. It may be possible to issue a subpoena directly to an employer or financial institution. A *subpoena* is a court order directing an individual or corporate representative to appear before the court or to produce documents in a pending lawsuit. In the discovery process, a subpoena is used to compel an individual or corporation to produce documents, papers, books, or other physical exhibits that constitute or contain evidence that is relevant to your case.

5.6   My spouse's attorney intends to subpoena my medical records. Aren't these private?

Whether or not your medical records are relevant in your case will depend upon the issues in dispute. If you are requesting alimony or if your health is an issue in the dispute of child custody, these records may be relevant.

Talk with your attorney about your rights. There are a number of options that may be available to prevent the disclosure of your information.

5.7   I own my business, will I have to disclose my business records?

Yes. You may be required to provide extensive records of your business in the discovery process. However, it is common for the court to protect the confidentiality of these records.

5.8   It's been two months since my attorney sent interrogatories to my spouse, and we still don't have his answers. I answered mine on time. Is there anything that can be done to speed up the process?

The failure or refusal of a spouse to follow the rules of discovery can add to both the frustration and expense of the divorce process. Talk with your attorney about filing a motion to compel discovery, seeking a court order that your spouse provides the requested information by a certain date. A request for attorney fees for the filing of the motion may also be appropriate.

Ask your attorney whether a subpoena of information from an employer or a financial institution would be a more cost-effective way to get needed facts and documents if your spouse remains uncooperative.

5.9   What is a *deposition*?

A *deposition* is the asking and answering of questions under oath, outside court, in the presence of a court reporter. A deposition may be taken of you, your spouse, or potential witnesses in your divorce case, including experts. Both attorneys will be present. You and your spouse also have the right to be present during the taking of depositions of any witnesses in your case. Depositions are not performed in every divorce case. They are most common in cases involving contested custody, complex financial issues, and expert witnesses.

After your deposition is completed, the questions and answers will be transcribed (typed) by the court reporter exactly as given and bound into one or more volumes.

5.10   What is the purpose of a deposition?

A deposition can serve a number of purposes such as:

- Supporting the settlement process by providing valuable information
- Helping your attorney determine who to use as witnesses at trial
- Aiding in the assessment of a witness' credibility, that is, whether the witness appears to be telling the truth
- Helping avoid surprises at the trial by learning the testimony of witnesses in advance
- Preserving testimony in the event the witness becomes unavailable for trial

Depositions can be essential tools in a divorce, especially when a case is likely to proceed to trial.

5.11   Will what I say in my deposition be used against me when we go to court?

Usually, a deposition is used to develop trial strategy and obtain information in preparation for trial. In some circumstances, a deposition may be used at trial.

If you are called later to testify as a witness and you give testimony contrary to your deposition, your deposition can be used to *impeach* you by showing the inconsistency in your statements. It is important to review your deposition prior to your live testimony to ensure consistency and prepare yourself for the type of questions you may be asked.

5.12   Will the judge read the depositions?

Unless a witness becomes unavailable for trial or gives conflicting testimony at trial, it is unlikely that the judge will ever read the depositions.

5.13   How should I prepare for my deposition?

To prepare for your deposition, review all the important documents in your case, such as the petition for dissolution of marriage, motions, your answers to interrogatories, your responses to requests for production, your financial affidavit, and any temporary hearing affidavits.

Gather all documents you've been asked to provide at your deposition. Deliver them to your attorney in advance of your deposition for copying and review. Talk to your attorney about the type of questions you can expect to be asked. Discuss with him or her any questions you are concerned about answering.

5.14   What will I be asked? Can I refuse to answer questions?

Questions in a deposition can cover a broad range of topics including your education, work, income, and family. The attorney is allowed to ask anything that is reasonably calculated to lead to the discovery of admissible evidence. If the question may lead to relevant information, it can be asked in a deposition, even though it may be inadmissible at trial. If you are unsure whether to answer a question, ask your attorney and follow his/her advice.

Your attorney also may object to inappropriate questions. If there is an objection, say nothing until the attorneys discuss the objection. You will be directed whether or not to answer.

5.15 What if I give incorrect information in my deposition?

You will be under oath during your deposition, so it is very important that you be truthful. If you give incorrect information by mistake, contact your attorney as soon as you realize the error. If you lie during your deposition, you risk having your honesty questioned by the other attorney during your divorce trial. This could cause you to lose credibility with the court, rendering your testimony less valuable.

5.16 What if I don't know or can't remember the answer to a question?

You may be asked questions about which you have no knowledge. It is always acceptable to say "I don't know" if you do not have the knowledge. Similarly, if you cannot remember, simply say so.

5.17 What else do I need to know about having my deposition taken?

The following suggestions will help you to give a successful deposition:

- Prepare for your deposition by reviewing and providing necessary documents and talking with your attorney.
- Get a good night's sleep the night before. Eat a meal with protein to sustain your energy, as the length of depositions can vary.
- Arrive early for your deposition so that you have time to get comfortable with your surroundings.
- Relax. You are going to be asked questions about matters you're familiar with. Your deposition is likely to begin with routine matters such as your educational and work history.
- Tell the truth, including whether you have met with an attorney or discussed preparation for the deposition.
- Stay calm. Your spouse's attorney will be judging your credibility and demeanor. Do not argue with the attorneys.

- Listen carefully to the entire question. Do not try to anticipate questions or start thinking about your answer before the attorney has finished asking the question.

- Answer the question directly. If the question calls only for "yes" or "no," provide such an answer.

- Do not volunteer information. If the attorney wants to elicit more information, he or she will do so in following questions.

- If you do not understand the question clearly, ask that it be repeated or rephrased. Do not try to answer the question you *think* was asked.

- Take your time and carefully consider the question before answering. There is no need to hurry.

- If you do not know or cannot remember the answer, say so. That is an adequate answer.

- Do not guess. If your answer is an estimate or approximation, say so. Do not let an attorney pin you down to anything you are not sure about. For example, if you cannot remember the number of times an event occurred, say that. If the attorney asks you if it was more than ten times, answer only if you can. If you can provide a range (more than ten but less than twenty) with reasonable certainty, you may do so.

- If an attorney mischaracterizes something you said earlier, say so.

- Speak clearly and loudly enough for everyone to hear you.

- Answer all questions with words, rather than gestures or sounds. "Uh-huh" is difficult for the court reporter to distinguish from "unh-unh" and may result in inaccuracies in the transcript.

- If you need a break at any point in the deposition, you have the right to request one. You can talk to your attorney during such a break.

- In advance of your deposition, discuss with your attorney whether you should review the transcript of your deposition for its accuracy or whether you should waive your right to review and sign the deposition.

Remember that the purpose of your deposition is to support a good outcome in your case. Completing it will help your case to move forward.

5.18 Are depositions always necessary? Does every witness have to be deposed?

Depositions are less likely to be needed if you and your spouse are reaching an agreement on most of the facts in your case and you are moving toward a settlement. They are more likely to be needed in cases where child custody is disputed or where there are complex financial issues. Although depositions of all witnesses are usually unnecessary, it is common to take depositions of expert witnesses.

5.19 Will I get a copy of the depositions in my case?

Ask your attorney for copies of the depositions in your case. It will be important for you to carefully review your deposition if your case proceeds to trial.

6

Mediation, Negotiation, and Collaboration

If your marriage is full of conflict, you might be asking how you can make the fighting stop. You picture your divorce as having vicious attorneys, an angry spouse, and screaming matches. You wonder if there is a way out of this nightmare.

Or, perhaps you and your spouse are parting ways amicably. Although you are in disagreement about how your divorce should be settled, you are clear that you want the process to be respectful and hostility-free. You'd rather spend your hard-earned money on your children's college education than on legal fees.

In either case, going to trial and having a judge make all of the decisions in your divorce is not inevitable. In fact, most New Mexico divorce cases settle without the need for a trial. The processes of mediation, negotiation, and collaboration can help you and your spouse to resolve your disputed issues and to reach your own agreements without taking your case before the judge who will make the decisions for you.

Resolving your divorce through a mediated, negotiated, or collaborated settlement has many advantages. You can achieve a mutually satisfying agreement, have a known outcome with little risk of appeal, and often enjoy significantly lower legal fees. Despite the circumstances that led to the end of your marriage, it might be possible for your divorce to conclude peacefully with the help of these tools.

6.1 What is the difference between *mediation* and *negotiation*?

Both mediation and negotiation are methods used to help you and your spouse settle your divorce by reaching a written agreement rather than going to trial and having the judge make decisions for you. These methods are sometimes referred to as *alternative dispute resolution (ADR)*.

In the *mediation* process, spouses hire a trained mediator who acts as an independent, neutral third party. He or she is a skilled professional who can assist you and your spouse in reaching agreements about different issues in your case. Either the mediator or attorneys for the parties draft the settlement document. Attorneys for the parties may also be present during mediation, although their involvement is usually less than in negotiation.

In the *negotiation* process, there is no neutral third party involved, but the two attorneys work out a settlement through the exchange of proposals, either verbally or in writing. They then draft a written document that contains the terms of the negotiated settlement. Often, a litigated case will become a negotiated settlement when, right before trial, one of the attorneys makes an offer and the other side either accepts the offer or makes a counteroffer that is ultimately accepted.

6.2 How are mediation and negotiation different from *collaboration*?

Collaborative divorce is a method of resolving a divorce case where both parties have a strong commitment to settling their disputes and avoiding litigation. You and your spouse each hire an attorney trained in the collaborative law process. You and your attorneys enter into a written agreement (referred to as the *disqualification agreement*) that provides that in the event either you or your spouse decides to take the case to court, both of you must terminate your representation by your collaborative attorneys and both parties must start anew with litigation attorneys.

Spouses in the collaborative process enlist the support of other professionals, such as an independent financial advisor, a child specialist, or a communication coach, to support them through the process. The collaboration process is a series of meetings that continue until a settlement is reached. The time it takes to reach the settlement may be quick or lengthy, depending upon the pace determined by the spouses themselves. This process enables the focus to shift away from the conflict and toward finding solutions. The attorneys become a part of the team supporting settlement rather than advocates adding to the conflict. All of the professional team members focus on finding a solution that ultimately results in a financial plan for each spouse and the children going forward.

Ask your attorney about whether or not your case would be well suited to the collaborative law process.

6.3 What is involved in the mediation process? What will I have to do and how long will it take?

The mediation process will be explained to you in detail by the mediator at the start of the mediation session. Mediation involves one or more meetings with you, your spouse, and the mediator. In some cases, the attorneys for each of you will also be present.

Prior to meeting with you and your spouse in an initial mediation session, the mediator will conduct an individual initial screening session with each of you to assess your ability to communicate with each other and to screen for domestic abuse or other forms of intimidation or coercion. After the mediator's initial screening, he or she will decide whether you and your spouse should mediate together, or whether your mediation should take place separately.

The mediator will outline ground rules designed to ensure that you will be treated respectfully and given an opportunity to be heard. In most cases, you and your spouse will each be given an opportunity to make some opening remarks about what is important to you in the outcome of your divorce.

How long the process of mediation continues depends upon many of the same factors that affect how long your divorce will take. These include how many issues you and your spouse disagree about, the complexity of these issues, and the willingness of each of you to work toward an agreement.

Your case could settle after just a couple of mediation sessions, or it might require a series of meetings. It is common for the mediator to clarify at the close of each session whether the parties are willing to continue with another session.

6.4 My attorney said that mediation/negotiation/collaboration can reduce delays in completing my divorce. How can these methods do this?

When the issues in your divorce are decided by a judge instead of by you and your spouse, there are many opportunities for delay. These can include:

- Waiting for the trial date
- Having to return to court on a later, second date if your trial is not completed on the first day it is scheduled
- Waiting for the judge's ruling on your case
- Needing additional court hearings after your trial to resolve disputes about the intention of the judge's rulings, issues that were overlooked, or disagreement regarding the language of the final decree of dissolution of marriage

Each one of these events holds the possibility of delaying your divorce by days, weeks, or even months. Mediating, negotiating, or collaborating regarding the terms of your final decree of dissolution of marriage can eliminate these delays.

6.5 How can mediation/negotiation/collaboration lower the costs of my divorce?

If your case is not settled by agreement, you will be going to trial. If the issues in your case are many or if they are complex, such as valuation of a business or contested custody, the attorney's fees and other costs of going to trial can be tremendous.

By settling your case without going to trial, you may be able to save thousands of dollars in legal fees. Ask your attorney for a litigation budget estimate that sets forth the potential costs of going to trial, so that you have some idea of these costs when deciding whether to settle an issue or to take it to trial before the judge.

6.6 Are there other benefits to mediating/negotiating/ collaborating a settlement?

Yes. A divorce resolved by a mediated, negotiated, or collaborated agreement can have these additional benefits:

- *Recognizing common goals.* Mediation, negotiation, and collaboration allow for brainstorming between the parties and attorneys. Looking at all possible solutions, even the impractical ones, invites creative solutions to common goals. For example, suppose you and your spouse both agree that you need to pay your spouse some amount of equity for the family home you will keep, but you have no cash to make the payment. Together, you might come up with a number of options for accomplishing your goal and select the best one. Contrast this with the judge who simply orders one spouse to pay the other a certain amount of money without considering all of the possible options.

- *Addressing the unique circumstances of your situation.* Rather than using a one-size-fits-all approach as a judge might do, a settlement reached by agreement allows you and your spouse to consider the unique circumstances of your situation in formulating a good outcome. For example, suppose you disagree about the parenting times for the Thanksgiving holiday. The judge might order you to alternate the holiday each year, even though you both would have preferred to have your child share the day.

- *Creating a safe place for communication.* These *alternative dispute resolution (ADR)* processes give each party an opportunity to be heard. Perhaps you and your spouse have not yet had an opportunity to share directly your concerns about settlement. For example, you might be worried about how the temporary parenting time arrangement is impacting your children, but have not yet talked to your spouse about it. A mediation, settlement conference, or collaborative session can be a safe place for you and your spouse to communicate your concerns about your children or your finances.

- *Fulfilling your children's needs.* You may see that your children would be better served by having you and your spouse deciding their future rather than having it decided by a judge who does not know, love, and understand your children like the two of you do.

- *Eliminating the risk and uncertainty of trial.* If a judge decides the outcome of your divorce, you give up control over the terms of the settlement. The decisions are left in the hands of the judge. If you and your spouse reach agreement, however, you have the power to eliminate the risk of an uncertain outcome.

- *Reducing the risk of harm to your children.* If your case goes to trial, it is likely that you and your spouse will give testimony that will be upsetting to each other. As the conflict increases, the relationship between you and your spouse inevitably deteriorates. This can be harmful to your children. Contrast this with mediation, settlement negotiations, or collaboration, in which you commit to being open with your communication and seek to reach agreement. Particularly in the collaborative process, it is not unusual for the relationship between the parents to improve as the professionals create a safe environment for rebuilding communication and reaching agreements in the best interest of a child.

- *Having the support of professionals.* Using trained professionals, such as mediators and attorneys, to support you can help you reach a settlement that you might think is impossible. These professionals have skills to help you focus on what is most important to you, and shift your attention away from irrelevant facts. They understand the law and know the possible outcomes if your case goes to trial.

- *Lowering stress.* The process of preparing for and going to court can be stressful. Your energy is also going toward caring for your children, looking at your finances, and coping with the emotions of divorce. You might decide that you would be better served by settling your case rather than proceeding to trial.

- *Achieving closure.* When you are going through a divorce, the process can feel as though it is taking an eternity. By reaching agreement, you and your spouse are better able to put the divorce behind you and move forward with your lives.

6.7   Is mediation mandatory?

No. Mediation is not required prior to filing for divorce in New Mexico, nor is mediation mandatory after a divorce has been filed to resolve the issues in the divorce. Mediation may be required within a particular judicial district by local court rule or by a judge as a matter of custom prior to allowing the parties to receive a trial setting. Talk to your attorney if you and your spouse have reached an agreement regarding any aspect of the case, such as a time-sharing schedule or the division of the furniture and personal property, as it is always possible to mediate portions of the divorce while reserving other parts to be decided by the court. For example, a couple might agree on the custody and time-sharing schedule for their children but cannot agree on the division of the assets and debts.

6.8   My spouse abused me and I am afraid to participate in mediation or collaboration. Should I participate anyway?

If you have been a victim of domestic violence by your spouse, it is important that you discuss the appropriateness of mediation or collaboration with your attorney. These methods may not be a safe way for you to reach agreement.

Prior to allowing either process to proceed, any mediator should ask you whether or not you have been a victim of domestic violence. This is critical for the mediator to both assess your safety and to ensure that the balance of power in the mediation process is maintained.

Talk with your attorney if you have experienced domestic violence or if you feel threatened or intimidated by your spouse. If so, your case may be referred to an approved specialized mediator for parents involved in high-conflict situations. It may be possible to mediate with you and your spouse in different rooms or during separate sessions.

If you feel threatened or intimidated by your spouse but still want to proceed with mediation, talk to your attorney about attending the mediation sessions with you. Request to have the mediation occur at your attorney's office, where you feel more comfortable. If you do participate in mediation, insist that your mediator have a good understanding of the dynamics of domestic abuse and how they can impact the mediation process.

In the collaboration process, your attorney will make sure that the divorce coach (a psychologist or therapist who is a neutral team member) is aware of the history of abuse. The coach will help both the parties and the attorneys insure that there is a balance of power and that the meetings are conducted in a safe manner. It may be that more "caucus" (i.e., one side only with the neutral financial coach and divorce coach) meetings occur instead of all parties, attorneys and coaches meeting together, if the dynamics are preventing a fair and balanced process.

6.9 What training and credentials do mediators/collaborative attorneys have?

The background of mediators varies. Some are attorneys; many come from other backgrounds such as counseling. Some are retired judges. Some mediators have received their training through the University of New Mexico and State Bar of New Mexico; others were trained out of state. Ask your attorney for help in finding a qualified mediator who has completed training in mediating family law cases. The availability of mediators also varies, depending upon where you live. Regional mediation centers are located throughout New Mexico, and many will travel to areas outside the Albuquerque/Santa Fe area.

To conduct collaborative divorces, attorneys must have attained a minimum amount of training hours, which are provided both in New Mexico and outside the state. To find a trained collaborative attorney or trained coaches, go to: www.collaborativepractice.com.

This website is a wealth of information about the attorneys and coaches in New Mexico.

6.10 What types of issues can be resolved through mediation or negotiation or through the collaborative process?

All of the issues in your case can be resolved through mediation, negotiation, or the collaborative divorce process. However, in advance of any mediation, collaborative, or negotiation session, you should discuss with your attorney if you should address all of the issues or just some of the issues through these ADR processes.

Always talk with your attorney in advance of any mediation about which issues or items you would like to see resolved outside the courtroom. You may decide that certain issues are nonnegotiable for you. Discuss this with your attorney in advance of any mediation or negotiation sessions so that he or she can support you in focusing the discussions on the issues you are open to looking at.

6.11 What is the role of my attorney in the mediation process?

The role of your attorney in the mediation process will vary depending upon which ADR process you are using. If you are attending mediation with your spouse and a neutral mediator but without your attorney, your attorney can assist you ahead of time in identifying which issues you want to be discussed in mediation and which ones are better left to negotiation between the attorneys, or left for the judge to decide. In all cases, it is important that your attorney review any agreements discussed in mediation before a final agreement is reached on any topic.

If you are attending a settlement facilitation in which both attorneys are present, along with the parties and a neutral facilitator, your attorney will represent you in the ongoing negotiations and, when offers are brought to you by the facilitator from the opposing side, will advise you to evaluate the pros and the cons of each offer and assist you in making a counteroffer, if appropriate.

If you are in a collaborative divorce, the role of the attorney is to guide the process. The attorneys will keep minutes from each meeting and set the agenda for the next meeting. The attorneys will assist the parties in conjunction with the financial neutral coach in coming up with a plan that works for both parties and the children.

6.12   How do I prepare for mediation?

Prior to attending a mediation session with your spouse, discuss with your attorney the issues you intend to mediate. Enlist your attorney's support in identifying your intentions for the mediation. Remember your list of goals for your divorce you compiled from Chapter 2. What are your most important goals for the process? Make a list of issues that help you attain your goals and that are important to you. For example, when it comes to your child, you might consider whether it is your child's safety, the parenting time schedule, or the ability to attend your children's events which concerns you most.

Be forward looking. Giving thought to your ultimate goals while approaching mediation with an open mind and heart is the best way to move closer to settlement.

6.13   Do children attend the mediation sessions?

Almost never. In most cases your child will not participate in the mediation. If a child's input is needed, there are different ways of hearing and addressing the children's needs depending on the type of process. There will be a "child specialist coach" if you are in a collaborative process, who will have met with the children and will report to both parents and the team what the children's needs are. If there has been a child-custody evaluation—a psychological evaluation of both parents and the child/children with a recommendation by the child psychologist serving as an expert witness—the child psychologist may attend the settlement facilitation or mediation and again speak to how to best meet the children's individual needs.

If you think your child's voice should be heard at the mediation table, talk to your attorney and your mediator or the collaborative team about the best method to do this.

6.14 I want my attorney to look over the agreements my spouse and I discussed in mediation before I give my final approval. Is this possible?

Yes. Before giving your written or final approval to any agreements reached in mediation, it is critical that your attorney review the agreements first. This is necessary to ensure that you understand the terms of the settlement and its implications. Your attorney will also review the agreement for compliance with New Mexico law.

6.15 Who pays for mediation or collaboration?

The cost of either process must be paid for by you or your spouse. Often, because the cost is paid from joint or community assets, each spouse is sharing the expense equally. Expect your mediator, your attorney, or the collaborative team to address the matter of fees before or at your first session.

6.16 What if mediation or collaborative process fails?

If mediation or the collaborative process is not successful at getting you to a full settlement on all issues, you still may be able to settle your case through negotiations between the attorneys. Also, you and your spouse can agree to preserve the settlements that were reached and to take only the remaining disputed issues to the judge for trial.

6.17 What is a *settlement conference* or a *settlement facilitation*?

A *settlement conference* or *settlement facilitation* can be a powerful tool for the resolution of your case. It is a meeting held with you, your spouse, and both attorneys with the intention of negotiating the terms of your divorce. In some cases, a professional with important information needed to support the settlement process, such as an accountant or financial planner, also may participate.

Settlement conferences are most effective when both parties and their attorneys see the potential for a negotiated resolution, and have the necessary information to accomplish that goal.

6.18 Why should I consider a settlement conference or facilitation when the attorneys can negotiate through letters and phone calls?

A settlement conference can eliminate the delays that often occur when negotiation takes place through correspondence and calls between the attorneys. Rather than waiting days or weeks for a response, you can receive a response on a proposal in a matter of minutes.

A settlement conference also enables you and your spouse, if you so choose, to use your own words to explain the reasoning behind your requests. You are also able to provide information immediately to expedite the process.

6.19 How do I prepare for my settlement conference or settlement facilitation?

Being well prepared for the settlement conference can help you make the most of this opportunity to resolve your case without the need to go to trial. Actions you should take include:

- Provide in advance of the conference all necessary information. If your attorney has asked you for a current pay stub, tax return, asset values, debt amounts, or other documentation, make sure it is provided prior to the meeting.

- Discuss your goals and your topics of concern with your attorney in advance. Your attorney can assist you in understanding your rights under the law so that you can have realistic expectations for the outcome of negotiations.

- Bring a positive attitude, a listening ear, and an open mind. Come with the attitude that your case will settle. Be willing to first listen to the opposing party, and then to share your position. To encourage your spouse to listen to your position, listen to hers or his first. Resist the urge to interrupt.

Few cases settle without each side demonstrating flexibility and a willingness to compromise. Most cases settle when the parties are able to bring these qualities to the process.

6.20 What will happen at my settlement conference or settlement facilitation?

Typically the conference will be held at the office of one of the attorneys, with both parties and attorneys present. If there are a number of issues to be discussed, an agenda may be used to keep the focus on relevant topics. From time to time throughout the conference, you and your attorney may meet alone to consult as needed. If additional information is needed to reach agreement, some issues may be set aside for later discussion.

The length of the conference depends upon the number of issues to be resolved, the complexity of the issues, and the willingness of the parties and attorneys to communicate effectively. An effort is made to confirm which issues are resolved and which issues remain disputed. Then, one by one the issues are addressed.

6.21 What is the role of my attorney in the settlement conference?

Your attorney is your advocate during the settlement conference. You can count on him or her to support you throughout the process, to see that important issues are addressed, and to counsel you privately outside the presence of your spouse and his/her attorney.

6.22 Why is my attorney appearing so friendly with my spouse and her attorney?

Successful negotiations rely upon building trust between the parties working toward agreement. Your attorney may be respectful or pleasant toward your spouse or your spouse's attorney for the purpose of promoting a good outcome for you.

6.23 What happens if my spouse and I settled some but not all of the issues in our divorce?

You and your spouse can agree to maintain the agreements you have reached and let the judge decide those matters that you are unable to resolve. In addition, if the day has been productive, the parties and attorneys may agree to return for another day or half day of settlement conference or facilitation if there is a realistic chance that with more time, a full agreement on all issues could be reached.

6.24   If my spouse and I reach an agreement, how long will it take before it can be finalized?

If a settlement is reached through negotiation or mediation or collaboration, one of the attorneys will put the agreement in writing in the form of a marital settlement agreement and final decree of dissolution of marriage for approval by you and your spouse. If both parties and both attorneys find the draft is acceptable, everyone will sign and then, most often, the document is delivered to the assigned judge. In most judicial districts in New Mexico, there is no need for an in-person appearance. However, all local rules should be consulted, and the judge's office will confirm if either or both parties must appear for the documents to be approved and filed. Once the marital settlement agreement and final decree of dissolution of marriage are filed, you are divorced. There is no waiting period in New Mexico as exists in some other states.

7

Emergency:
When You Fear Your Spouse

Divorce can be very emotional and may cause even the most rational people to act in inappropriate ways. People often panic over the thought of losing their family or their financial stability. If a situation was already volatile, divorce also can be the final straw for many people. It is not unusual for people to make threats, to steal money, to destroy property, or to hide children from the other parent.

When facing such emergencies, attempt to remain calm and take appropriate action to protect yourself, your children, and your assets. If children are involved, it is important to their future development that they are not in the middle of a violent situation and that they feel some level of security with at least one of their parents. When facing an emergency, do your best to focus on what to do in the immediate moment to not make the situation worse. New Mexico law provides many remedies that can help in this type of a situation.

7.1 I'm afraid my abusive spouse will try to hurt me and/ or our children if I say I want a divorce. What can I do legally to protect myself and my children?

Develop a plan with your safety and that of your children as your highest priority. In addition to meeting with an attorney at your first opportunity, develop a safety plan in the event you and your children need to escape your home. Your risk of harm from an abusive spouse increases when you leave. For this reason, all actions must be taken with safety as the first concern.

Consult with an agency that helps victims of domestic violence. Call the National Domestic Violence Hot-line at (800) SAFE (7233), the Women Against Violence Hot-line at (800) 799-7233, or the New Mexico Coalition Against Domestic Violence at (505) 246-9240 to get more information about the domestic violence program closest to you. And, of course, in case of emergency, call 911.

It is important that you find an attorney who understands domestic violence. Often your local domestic violence agency can help with a referral. Talk to your attorney about the concerns for your safety and that of your children. Ask your attorney about an order of protection, sometimes referred to as a temporary restraining order. This is a court order that may offer a number of protections including granting you temporary custody of your children for a limited time period, ordering your spouse to leave the family residence, ordering your spouse to stay away from your workplace, setting temporary support, and restraining your spouse from contacting you.

You can seek an order of protection without an attorney as well. If you feel you need such an order, contact your local district court clerk to find out the procedure for obtaining such an order without an attorney. Generally this involves completing a sworn application for the order of protection that details the acts of domestic violence.

7.2   I am afraid to meet with an attorney because I am terrified that my spouse will find out and get violent. What should I do?

Schedule an initial consultation with an attorney who is experienced in working with domestic violence victims. When you schedule the appointment, let the firm know your situation and instruct the law office not to place any calls to you that your spouse might discover. If you think your calls or e-mails are being monitored, make the call or contact from someone else's phone or computer. If your finances are being monitored, you should consider paying for your consultation in a way that cannot be traced. If possible, schedule your consultation in the morning in case the attorney advises you to immediately seek an order of protection. In this situation, you can go straight from the attorney's office to the court to apply for one.

Give your attorney all of the details regarding your fears and any acts of violence or abuse. An attorney cannot advise you without knowing the full story. If you take no action because you fear the consequences, nothing will change for you. It is not easy to take that first step to break the cycle of violence, but it is the only avenue for a new life for you and for your children. Consultations with your attorney are confidential. Your attorney has an ethical duty to not disclose your meeting to anyone outside the law firm. Let your attorney know your concerns so that extra precautions can be taken by the law office in handling your file.

7.3   I want to give my attorney all the information needed so my children and I are safe from my spouse. What does this include?

Provide your attorney with complete information about the history, background, nature, and evidence of your abuse including:

- The types of abuse (for example, physical, sexual, verbal, financial, mental, emotional)
- A description of the specifics of any acts of abuse or violence, including the dates, locations, and what happened
- Whether you were ever treated medically for injuries related to abuse, and if any records of that treatment exist
- Any police reports made or prior arrests for any crimes
- Evidence of the abuse (pictures, e-mails, letters, notes, or journal entries)
- Any witnesses to the abuse
- Any statements made by your spouse admitting the abuse
- Any known abuse of others, such as former spouses, significant others, children, or pets
- Alcohol or drug abuse by your spouse
- The possession of guns or other weapons by your spouse.

The better the information you provide to your attorney, the easier it will be for him/her to make a strong case for the protection of you and your children.

7.4   I'm not ready to hire an attorney for a divorce, but I am afraid my spouse is going to get violent with my children and me in the meantime. What can I do?

You do not need to file a divorce action to obtain an order of protection. It is possible to seek an order of protection from the court without an attorney and without filing for divorce. It is possible for the judge to order your spouse out of your home, to grant you custody of your children for a limited time, and to order your spouse to stay away from you, your home, and your work and to provide for temporary support as part of this order.

7.5   What's the difference between a *domestic abuse order of protection* and a *temporary restraining order*?

The names of orders and the procedures for obtaining them can differ from place to place and may change over time. Protection orders and restraining orders are both court orders directing a person to not engage in certain behavior. Both of these orders are intended to protect others. While either order can initially be obtained without notice to the other person (referred to as an *ex parte* order), that person always has a right to a hearing to determine whether or not an order of protection or a restraining order should remain in place beyond the initial temporary period. If a hearing determines that the order should continue beyond the initial temporary period, it will only be extended for a set period of time. If a valid need for protection still exists after that extended period of time, a person may generally apply for a further extension of the order.

Practice and procedure varies from county to county in New Mexico. A domestic violence *order of protection* can be obtained if the applicant and the adverse party are household members. "Household members" can be a misleading term, because it is not necessary that the parties actually share a home or cohabit. Household members are spouses, former spouses, parents, present or former stepparents, grandparents, grandparent-in-laws, children, stepchildren, grandchildren, co-parents, or individuals who share a dating or intimate relationship. An order of protection can be issued even if the acts of abuse did not involve physical harm or injury, but rather involved such things as severe emotional distress, a threat causing imminent fear of injury, trespass, damage to property, repeatedly driving by a residence or workplace, telephone harassment or other forms of harassment, or harm or threats of harm to children. If an order of protection is violated, the remedy is to call the police. They will immediately enforce the order by arresting the offending person if they believe there is probable cause to do so.

In contrast, a *temporary restraining order* is generally provided in a divorce action or a civil action and is not necessarily limited to acts of domestic abuse. Further, to enforce a temporary restraining order, a person generally must file a motion with the court alleging that the restraining order has been violated and then wait for a hearing on the motion to see if it will be enforced and what the potential sanctions may be.

Talk to your attorney about obtaining a domestic violence order of protection if you are concerned about your safety, your children's safety, or if there has been a history of domestic abuse. If your spouse has committed an act of abuse, as set forth above, you may qualify for a domestic violence order of protection. The violation of a domestic violence order of protection is a criminal offense, which can result in immediate arrest.

7.6 My spouse has never been violent, but I know he is going to be really angry and upset when the divorce papers are served. Do I need an order of protection?

The facts of your case may not warrant a protection order. Currently in New Mexico, when an action for divorce, paternity, or other family-related case is filed, the court issues a *temporary domestic order (TDO)* that is binding on the petitioner when the petition for dissolution of marriage is filed and is binding on the respondent when he or she is served with the petition for dissolution of marriage and the TDO. One of the provisions of the TDO directs both parties to not injure or physically or mentally abuse, molest, intimidate, threaten, or harass the other party or any child of either party while the divorce is in process. This TDO also includes provisions that order both parties not to sell, remove, transfer, dispose of, hide, encumber, or damage any property; not to interfere with the relationship of either party with the children; not to change beneficiaries on accounts and life insurance; and not to close any financial accounts or cancel any credit cards. This is in essence an order to maintain the status quo of the parties and is not an order of protection.

If you are concerned that actual service of the petition for dissolution of marriage, the TDO, and the summons will cause your spouse to become so angry that he or she may be threatening or dangerous to you, discuss the best mode of service with your attorney. Sometimes, people respond better if they are not served at work or if they can agree to pick up the documents from the other person's attorney.

If the act of receiving notice of the divorce proceeding so angers your spouse that they become threatening, harassing, or violent, inform your attorney immediately. It is possible to apply for and obtain an order of protection at any time during a divorce proceeding. Your attorney can help you decide if your spouse's behavior warrants applying for an order of protection. And, as always, if there is truly an emergency contact 911.

7.7 I'm afraid my spouse is going to take all of the money out of the bank accounts and leave me with nothing. What can I do?

Talk to your attorney immediately. If you are worried about your spouse emptying financial accounts or selling marital assets, it is critical that you take action at once. Your attorney can advise you on your right to take possession of certain assets in order to protect them from being hidden or spent by your spouse.

When the divorce is filed, a TDO is issued by the court that orders parties not to close any financial accounts or cancel any credit cards. If your spouse removes funds from accounts without your knowledge, your attorney can file a motion to enforce the TDO.

Also, ask your attorney about seeking a temporary restraining order or a preliminary injunction against your spouse. A temporary restraining order may forbid your spouse from taking money or assets without your agreement and from selling, transferring, hiding, or otherwise disposing of marital property until the divorce is complete. A *preliminary injunction* is a request to have the court take action to stop someone from doing something before they have done it. In this instance, the intent would be to prevent assets from disappearing and to maintain the status quo before a final division of the property from your marriage is complete. If this is a concern, talk to your attorney about the benefits of obtaining a temporary restraining order for property prior to giving your spouse notice that you are filing for divorce. It is much easier to prevent assets from disappearing then to try to track them down later but it is important to make sure that your claims are credible so that the court does not see you as the person attempting to gain control over your spouse.

7.8   If either my spouse or I file for divorce, will I be ordered out of my home? Who decides who gets to live in the house while we go through the divorce?

At the onset of the case, when a petition for dissolution of marriage is filed, the court issues a TDO that provides neither party shall make the other leave the family home, whether it be community or separate property, without a court order. It further directs that the parties should attempt to resolve the question of who leaves the home in a fair manner. If you and your spouse cannot reach an agreement regarding which of you will leave the residence during the divorce, a court will decide whether one of you should be granted exclusive possession of the home until the case is concluded. In some cases, especially when there is no financial ability to provide for two residences, judges have been known to refuse to order either party out of the house until the divorce is concluded.

Abusive behavior is one basis for seeking temporary possession of the home. If there are minor children, the custodial parent will ordinarily be awarded temporary possession of the residence.

Other factors the judge may consider include:

- Whether one of you owned the home prior to the marriage

- Who can afford to remain in the home or obtain other housing after provisions are made for payment of temporary support
- Who is most likely to be awarded the home in the divorce
- Options available to each of you for other temporary housing, including other homes or family members who live in the area
- Special needs that would make a move unduly burdensome, such as a health condition
- Self-employment from home, which could not be readily moved, such as a child-care business

If staying in the home is important to you, talk to your attorney about your reasons so that a strong case can be made for you at the temporary hearing.

7.9   My spouse says that I am crazy, that I am a liar, and that no judge will ever believe me if I tell the truth about the abusive behavior. What can I do if I don't have any proof?

It is very common for persons who abuse others to claim that their victims are liars and to make statements intended to discourage disclosure of the abuse. This is yet another form of controlling behavior. Most domestic violence is not witnessed by third parties. Often there is little physical evidence. Even without physical evidence, such as pictures or police reports, a judge can enter orders to protect you and your children if you give truthful testimony about your abuse which the judge finds believable. Your own testimony of your abuse is evidence.

Your attorney's skills and experience will support you in giving effective testimony in the courtroom to establish your case. Let your attorney know your concerns so that a strong case can be presented to the judge based upon your persuasive statements of the truth of your experience.

7.10 My spouse told me that if I ever file for divorce, I'll never see my child again. Should I be worried about my child being abducted?

Your fear that your spouse will abduct your child is a common one. This type of threat itself may be a form of harassment that results in an entry of an order of protection. Although most threats are just that, it is serious enough that, although you should not panic, you should seriously consider some of the factors that appear to increase the risk that your child will be removed from the state by the other parent:

- Any history of prior abductions, attempted abductions, or threatened abductions
- Abandoning employment
- Selling a primary residence or other large asset or terminating a lease
- Closing bank accounts, liquidating assets, or hiding or destroying documents
- Applying for a passport or visa, or obtaining travel documents for the child or other person
- Any history of domestic violence, stalking, or child abuse or neglect
- Prior refusal to obey child-custody or visitation orders
- An absence of strong family, emotional, or cultural ties in this state
- Strong ties to some other state or country, particularly one that does not have laws requiring the return of kidnapped children
- Immigration or citizenship status difficulties of your spouse that might make it difficult to remain in New Mexico
- Your spouse has had an application for U.S. citizenship denied
- Your spouse has ever used forged or misleading documents to obtain a passport, visa, or driver's license
- Your spouse has used multiple names in an effort to mislead or commit fraud

The risk of child abduction appears more serious in relationships between parties that cross culture, race, religion, or ethnicity. A lower socioeconomic status, prior criminal record, and limited social or economic ties to the community can also increase risk.

Programming and brainwashing are almost always present in cases where a child is at risk for being kidnapped by a parent, and efforts to isolate the child may also be seen. Exit activities such as obtaining a new passport, getting financial matters in order, or contacting a moving company could be indicators.

Talk to your attorney to assess the risks in your particular case. Together you can determine whether statements by your spouse are threats intended to control or intimidate you or whether legal action is needed to protect your child.

7.11 What legal steps can be taken to prevent my spouse from removing our child from the state or the country?

A permanent move or relocation is different from the concern that a person will travel out of state with a child without permission of the other parent. The TDO that is issued when a petition for dissolution of marriage is filed orders both parties not to remove, cause, or permit the removal of any minor child of both parties from the State of New Mexico without a court order or written consent of the other party. If you are concerned about your child being removed from the state, ask your attorney whether any of these options might be available in your case:

- A court order giving you immediate custody until a temporary custody hearing can be held
- A court order directing your spouse to turn over passports for the child and your spouse to the court
- The posting of a bond prior to your spouse exercising parenting time
- Supervised visitation by your spouse
- Imposition of travel restrictions relating to the child
- A requirement to obtain orders or guarantees from the officials of other countries before visitation with the child is permitted

- Issuing a warrant to take physical custody of the child and directing law enforcement assistance

Both state and federal laws are designed to provide protection from the removal of children from one state to another when a custody matter is brought and to protect children from kidnapping. *The Uniform Child Custody Jurisdiction and Enforcement Act (UCCJEA)* was passed to encourage child custody to be decided in the state where they have been living most recently and where they have the most ties. There are also criminal laws, both state and federal, designed to deter and to punish kidnapping as well. For example, *The Parental Kidnapping Prevention Act (PKPA)* makes it a federal crime for a parent to kidnap a child in violation of a valid custody order.

In the event of international travel, try to secure your child's passport. You can also contact the U.S. Department of State at (888) 407-4747 and ask them about the State Department's Children's Passport Issuance Alert Program (CPIAP). The State Department can place an alert on your child's passport that notifies authorities that child does not have the permission of both parents to travel internationally.

If you are concerned about your child being abducted, talk with your attorney about all options available to you for your child's protection. If the issue is related to the relocation of the minor child with either parent out of state or to another country, that will be decided as part of the custody portion of your case.

8

Child Custody

Ever since you and your spouse began talking about divorce, chances are your children have been your greatest concern. You or your spouse might have postponed the decision to seek divorce because of concern about the impact on your children. Now that the time has come, you might still have doubts about whether or not your children will be all right after the divorce.

Remember that you have been making wise and loving decisions for your children since they were born. You've always done your best to see that they had everything they really needed. You loved them and protected them. This won't change because you are going through a divorce. You were a good parent before the divorce and you will be a good parent after the divorce.

It can be difficult not to worry about how sharing parenting time with your spouse will affect your child. You may also have fears about being cut out of your child's life. Try to remember that, regardless of who has custody, it is likely that a court order will not only give you a lot of time with your children but will also guarantee ample opportunity to be involved in their day-to-day lives.

With the help of your attorney, you can make sound decisions regarding custody arrangements that are in the best interest of your children.

8.1   What types of custody are awarded in New Mexico?

Under New Mexico law, there are two aspects to a custody determination. These are legal custody and physical custody. *Legal custody* refers to the power to make major decisions regarding your children, such as where they live, which school they attend, what religion they should be raised in, what recreational activities they will participate in, and who should provide their health care.

There is a presumption in New Mexico that joint legal custody is in the best interest of a child. This means that the court will award joint legal custody unless there is a compelling reason not to. *Joint legal custody* means that you and your former spouse will share equally in the major decisions regarding your child. If you and the other parent are unable to reach an agreement regarding one of the major areas of your child's life, you may not make a change without a court order. Oftentimes, the court will require you to attempt mediation before going to court for a decision.

Sole legal custody, where one parent is the primary and final decision maker for the major decisions regarding your children, is rarely ordered.

Physical custody, on the other hand, refers to the physical location of the children; that is, where they spend their time. Like legal custody, it may be awarded to either parent or to both parents jointly. *Joint physical custody* is sometimes referred to as *shared physical custody.* Notwithstanding who has legal custody, the parent who is with the children will make the day-to-day decisions regarding their care.

Specific parenting time will always be awarded to each parent, regardless of who has legal custody. Provisions for days of the week, school breaks, summer, holidays, and vacations are typically made in detail.

8.2   On what basis will the judge award custody?

In determining whether joint legal custody is in the best interest of the child, the court shall consider the following factors:

- Whether or not the child has established a close relationship with each parent.

- Whether each parent is capable of providing adequate care for the child throughout each period of responsibility, including arranging for the child's care by others as needed.
- Whether each parent is willing to accept all responsibilities of parenting, including the willingness to accept care of the child at specified times and to relinquish care to the other parent at specified times.
- Whether the child can maintain and strengthen a relationship with both parents through predictable, frequent contact and whether the child's development will profit from such involvement with and influence from both parents.
- Whether each parent is able to allow the other to provide care without intrusion, that is, to respect the other's parental rights and responsibilities and right to privacy.
- The suitability of the parenting plan for the implementation of joint custody, preferably, although not necessarily, one arrived at through parental agreement.
- Geographic distance between the parents' residences.
- Willingness or ability of the parents to communicate, cooperate, or agree on issues regarding the child's needs.
- Whether a judicial adjudication has been made in a prior or the present proceeding that either parent or other person seeking custody has engaged in one or more acts of domestic abuse against the child, a parent of the child, or other household member. If a determination is made that domestic abuse has occurred, the court shall set forth findings that the custody or visitation ordered by the court adequately protects the child, the abused parent, or other household member.

If the minor child is younger than the age of fourteen, the court shall determine custody in accordance with the best interest of the child. The court shall consider all relevant factors including, but not limited to:

- The wishes of the child's parent(s) as to his custody
- The wishes of the child as to his custodian
- The interaction and interrelationship of the child with his parents, his siblings, and any other person who may significantly affect the child's best interest
- The child's adjustment to his home, school, and community
- The mental and physical health of all individuals involved

It is also worth noting that if a minor is fourteen years of age or older, the court shall consider the desires of the minor as to whom he wishes to live before awarding custody of such minor. This is not to say that the court will rubber-stamp the child's wishes but it must consider them.

8.3   How will my spouse and I decide with whom the children will live during the divorce proceedings?

Ideally, you and your spouse, with the assistance of your attorneys, can work out a temporary time-sharing arrangement to be followed during the divorce proceedings. Once an agreement is reached, the attorneys will draft and file a temporary order with the court. Informal agreements between parties cannot always be relied upon and may not be able to be enforced by the court. If an agreement cannot be reached, a hearing can be requested and the judge will make a ruling regarding temporary custody and time-sharing.

8.4   How much weight does the child's preference carry in the court's decision?

Your child's age is only one of many factors a judge may consider in determining custody. Your child's age and his/her ability to express the underlying reason for their preference to live with either parent will determine the amount of weight the judge will give to your child's preference.

8.5 How can I prove that I was the primary caregiver during the marriage?

One tool to assist you and your attorney in establishing your case as a primary caregiver is a chart indicating the care you and your spouse have each provided for your child. The clearer you are about the parenting history, the better job your attorney can do in presenting your case to the judge. Consider the activities in the chart below to help you clarify your respective contributions as parents.

Parental Roles Chart

Activity	Mother	Father
Attended prenatal medical visits		
Attended prenatal classes		
Took time off work after child was born		
Got up with child for feedings		
Got up with child when sick at night		
Bathed child		
Put child to bed		
Potty-trained child		
Prepared and fed meals to child		
Helped child learn numbers, letters, colors		
Helped child with practice for sports, music, dance		
Took time off work for child's appointments		
Stayed home from work with sick child		
Took child to doctor visits		
Went to pharmacy for the child's medication		
Took child to therapy		
Took child to optometrist		
Took child to dentist		

Parental Roles Chart (Continued)

Activity	Mother	Father
Took child to get haircuts		
Bought clothing for child		
Bought school supplies for child		
Transported child to school		
Picked up child after school		
Drove carpool for child's school		
Attended child's school activities		
Helped child with homework and projects		
Attended parent–teacher conferences		
Helped in child's classroom		
Chaperoned child's school trips and activities		
Transported child to day care		
Attended day-care activities		
Signed child up for sports, music, dance		
Bought equipment for sports, music, dance		
Transported child to sports, music, dance		
Attended sports, music, dance practices		
Attended sports games, music, dance recital		
Coached the child's sports		
Transported child from sports, music, dance		
Knows child's friends and friends' families		
Took child to religious education		
Participated in child's religious education		
Obtained information and training about special needs of the child		
Comforted child during times of emotional upset		

8.6   Do I have to let my spouse see the children before we are actually divorced?

Unless your children are at risk of being harmed by your spouse, your children should maintain regular contact with the other parent. It is important for children to experience the presence of both parents in their lives, regardless of the separation of the parents. Even if there is no temporary order for parenting time, cooperate with your spouse in making reasonable arrangements for time with your children.

Regardless of whether you consider your spouse to be an inadequate parent, work with them to establish reasonable parenting time unless there are real concerns about the children's safety or welfare. If you deny contact with the other parent, your judge may question whether you have the best interest of your child at heart. Arguments such as "the kids don't want to see him" are rarely persuasive. Your willingness to promote the other parent's relationship is a factor that the court will consider in a contested custody case.

On the other hand, if your spouse makes demands for time that are excessive or disruptive to the children, don't automatically agree. Talk to your attorney about an appropriate temporary parenting schedule. Balance the children's need to see the other parent with their need for stability.

8.7   I am seeing a therapist. Will that hurt my chances of getting custody?

If you are seeing a therapist, commend yourself for getting the professional support you need. Your well-being is important to your ability to be the best parent you can be.

Discuss with your attorney the implications of your being treated by a therapist. It may be that the condition for which you are being treated in no way affects your child or your ability to be a loving and supportive parent.

Be aware, however, that your mental health records may be subpoenaed by the other parent's attorney. For this reason it is important to discuss with your attorney an action plan for responding to a request to obtain records in your therapist's file. Ask your attorney to contact your therapist to alert him/her regarding how to respond to a request for your mental health records.

8.8   I am taking prescription medication to treat my depression; will this hurt my chances of getting custody?

No. Feelings of depression, anxiety, and trouble sleeping are common during a divorce. If you have any mental health concerns, seek help from a professional. Following through with the recommendations made by your health care provider will be looked upon favorably by the court. If medication is prescribed, the court will want to know that you are following the recommendations of your mental health professionals and taking your medication.

8.9   Will my children be present if we go to court?

In most instances, no. Judges make every effort to protect minor children from the conflict of their parents. For this reason, most judges will not allow children to be present in the courtroom to hear the testimony of other witnesses.

8.10   Should I hire a private detective to prove my spouse is having an affair?

It is rare to hire a private detective for this purpose. Proving an individual to be an unfit spouse does not prove them as an unfit parent. Your attorney can help you determine whether hiring a private investigator is a good idea in your particular case.

8.11   Will the fact that I had an affair during the marriage hurt my chances of getting custody?

An affair is unlikely to have a negative impact on custody. The standard for the court to consider is the best interest of the children, not whether or not you were a loyal spouse. Provided the affair did not negatively impact your ability to parent, or did not affect the children, it will likely be unimportant to the issue of custody. If, however, the children were exposed to the affair, or your parenting was affected by the affair—such as missing the children's events or neglecting them emotionally—the affair may impact the custody case.

8.12 During the months it takes to get a divorce, is it okay to date or will it hurt my chances at custody?

If custody is disputed, talk with your attorney about your plans to begin dating. Your dating may be irrelevant if the children are unaware of it. However, most judges will frown upon exposing your children to a new relationship when they are still adjusting to the separation of their parents. Even though you may be excited about a new romantic interest and want your children to meet this person, it is unnecessary and potentially harmful for your children.

The other thing to consider is that if your spouse discovers that the children have met this new person in your life, it may inflame an already volatile situation. For the sake of your children and your own interests, it's best to try to keep things as calm as possible during this difficult period.

8.13 I'm gay and came out to my spouse when I filed for divorce. What impact will my sexual orientation have on my case for custody or parenting time?

There are no laws in New Mexico that limit your rights as a parent based upon your sexual orientation. Your sexual orientation itself is unimportant; what's important is how that orientation impacts the children. Assuming your sexual orientation does not disrupt the children, it should make no difference in the case. You may want to speak with a child psychologist about the best way to approach this issue with your children.

Although you may be excited about finally embracing your true sexual orientation, this revelation may be devastating to your spouse. You may have struggled with the decision to come out for years, but your spouse might have only had a short amount of time to digest this information and its implications. Try to be sensitive and patient in the hopes that your spouse will soon respond in kind.

8.14 How is *abandonment* legally defined, and how might it affect the outcome of our custody battle?

Abandonment is rarely an issue in custody litigation unless one parent has been absent from the child's life for an extended period. Under New Mexico law, abandonment is a ground for divorce but the grounds for a divorce are generally irrelevant to the determination of custody.

8.15 Can I have witnesses speak on my behalf to try to get custody of my children?

Yes. Witnesses are critical in every custody case. It is important to determine early on which witnesses you will want to call upon to support your custody claims. Witnesses are not only important at trial but also before trial: they may speak to a guardian *ad litem* or a custody expert about your strengths as a parent and any problems with your spouse's parenting.

The best witnesses are those who don't have any bias. You can call a family member or close friend to testify about what a good parent you are but this testimony tends to be perceived as biased. A non-biased person such as one of the children's teachers or coaches usually provides more credible testimony because they are not usually aligned with either parent but can provide concrete information about the child and the parents.

In considering which witnesses would best support your case, your attorney may consider the following:

- Does the witness have any biases or prejudices that could impact the testimony?
- What is the relationship of the witness to the child and the parents?
- Has the witnessed observed the other parent with the child? If so, how frequently? How recently?
- How long has the witness known you or the other parent?
- Has the witness made inconsistent statements concerning any of the issues about which he/she will testify?
- How valuable is the knowledge of this witness?
- Does this witness have knowledge different from that of other witnesses?
- Is the witness available and willing to testify?
- Is the witness clear in conveying information?
- Is the witness credible? Will the judge believe this witness?

You and your attorney can work together to determine which witnesses will best support your case. Support your attorney by providing a list of potential witnesses together with their contact information and your opinion regarding the answers to the above questions.

Give your attorney the phone numbers, addresses, e-mail addresses, and workplace information for each of your potential witnesses. This information can be critical in interviewing the witnesses, contacting them regarding testifying, and issuing subpoenas to compel their court attendance if needed. When parents give conflicting testimony during a custody trial, the testimony of other witnesses can be key to determining the outcome of the case.

8.16   Will my attorney want to speak with my children?

It is a rare occasion for your attorney to ask to speak with your children. Information is typically gathered from children by either a guardian *ad litem* or a custody expert.

8.17   Who is a guardian *ad litem*? Why is one appointed?

In custody cases, a guardian *ad litem* is an individual who is appointed by the court to represent the best interest of the child. The guardian *ad litem* (commonly referred to as the GAL) is an attorney who is directed by the judge to conduct an investigation and issue a report and recommendations as to a custody and time-sharing arrangement in the best interest of the children.

8.18   What is a *child-custody expert*? Why is one appointed?

If custody is disputed, the court may order a *child-custody expert* be appointed. The child-custody expert, also known in New Mexico as a *Rule 11-706 expert,* is a neutral evaluator whose role is to determine the best interest of the child and to make recommendations to the court concerning custody and parenting time. The child-custody expert is typically a child psychologist who conducts a complete evaluation of the parties, conducts psychological testing, interviews the parents and the child, and evaluates the interaction between the child and both parents. The expert is also authorized to review and receive information, records, and reports concerning all parties involved from either party or any other non-biased witness. The expert will then submit a report to the court with his/her recommendations as to a custody and time-sharing arrangement in the best interest of the children. The custody expert can also be called as a witness at trial.

8.19 What information should I provide to the guardian *ad litem* or custody expert?

It is important to share information with the guardian *ad litem* or custody expert about your child's day-to-day life. This will help this individual learn more about your child's needs. If you are making an allegation about the other spouse, it is helpful to provide evidence substantiating this allegation. If your allegation is that the other spouse never takes or picks up the child from day care, it might be helpful to obtain copies of the daily sign-in and sign-out sheets for the last few months. If your allegation is that your spouse's behavior makes effective communication difficult, you might want to provide copies of e-mails or text messages reflecting your spouse's poor communication style.

Talk to your attorney about what information would be helpful in your case.

8.20 Why might I not be awarded sole physical custody?

Unless there is abuse or neglect, it is rare for the court to give a parent sole physical custody without some visitation with the other parent. It is almost universally in a child's best interest to have a relationship and spend time with both parents. The exception to this rule is if one or both of the parents is unfit to appropriately parent the child.

8.21 What does it mean to be an *unfit parent*?

Parental unfitness means that you have a personal deficiency or incapacity that will likely prevent you from performing essential parental obligations and is likely to result in a detriment to your child's well-being.

Determinations of your fitness to be a custodial parent will largely depend upon the facts of your case. Reasons why a parent might be found to be unfit include a history of physical abuse, alcohol or drug abuse, or untreated mental health problems that affect an individual's ability to parent.

8.22 Does joint physical custody always mean equal time at each parent's house?

No. Joint physical custody means that each parent has regular and predictable time-sharing with the child. In a joint physical custody situation, there is no presumption as to the amount of time each parent will have.

8.23 If I am awarded joint physical custody, what are some examples of how the parenting might be shared?

Time-sharing is often determined based on a child's age, stage of development, and the level of involvement each parent had with the child during the marriage. Custody experts tend to recommend that young children should live primarily with one parent with the other parent having frequent and predictable time-sharing with the child. It is rare for a custody expert to recommend a time-sharing arrangement in which a child goes without seeing either parent for a long stretch of time—the exception is, of course, when parents live in different states. As a child grows older, he can often tolerate being away from one parent for longer stretches of time.

There are hundreds of time-sharing arrangements that can work for you and your family. As a rule, unless the child is very young, child-custody experts like to minimize the number of times the child has to transition from one household to the other each week. For instance, arrangements where the child sleeps at a different house each night are frowned upon. Custody experts prefer to see arrangements where the child stays with a parent for blocks of time. As indicated above, the length of these time blocks is determined by the child's status quo, age, and stage of development. The specific time-sharing arrangement will usually be spelled out in a parenting plan and filed with the court.

8.24 What is a *parenting plan*?

A *parenting plan* is a document detailing how you and your spouse will parent your child after the divorce. Among the issues addressed in a parenting plan are:

113

- Custody, both legal and physical
- Parenting time, including specific times for:
  - The regular school year
  - Holidays
  - Birthdays
  - Mother's Day and Father's Day
  - Summer
  - School breaks
- Phone access to the child
- Communication with each other regarding the child
- Access to the child's records
- Notice regarding parenting time
- Attendance at the child's activities
- Decision making regarding the child
- Exchange of information such as addresses, phone numbers, and care providers
- How disputes will be handled

Detailed parenting plans provide clarity regarding each parent's rights and responsibilities. These agreements also provide security for the child by reducing parental conflict, which lowers the possibility of returning to court. Anything that reduces parental conflict ultimately benefits the child.

8.25 I don't think it's safe for my children to have any contact with my spouse. What are my options?

Keeping your children safe is of the utmost importance. If you have safety concerns for your children or yourself, you should discuss those concerns with your attorney right away. Your attorney can help develop a plan to protect you and your children. Options might include an order of protection, supervised visitation, or certain restrictions on your spouse's parenting time.

Be aware that the law imposes a strict burden on a parent seeking to restrict the other parent's access to the children. The law presumes it is in the best interest of children to have a relationship with both parents. In order to limit your spouse's access to the children, you must prove there is a substantial risk of harm to the children if protections are not implemented. Convincing evidence is necessary to restrict another parent's visitation or access to the children.

Give your attorney a complete history of the facts upon which you base your belief that your children are not safe with the other parent. Although the most recent facts are often the most relevant, it is important that your attorney have a clear picture of the background as well. Concrete examples of past abuse or neglect will be required. Vague or intuitive concerns about child safety will not be sufficient to limit access. It is a good idea to make a list detailing all incidents in which you believe your spouse was abusive or neglectful. Give this information to your attorney so he or she can evaluate the strength of your claims

Your attorney also needs information about your spouse, such as whether your spouse is or has been:

- Using alcohol or drugs
- Treated for alcohol or drug use
- Arrested, charged, or convicted of crimes of violence
- In possession of firearms
- Subject to a protection order for harassment or violence

Assuming that you have sufficient evidence to support your concern about the children's safety, the judge has a number of remedies available. One such remedy is for visitation between your spouse and the children to be supervised. Supervised visitation allows a parent to exercise their parenting time under the supervision of another person. This allows the parent access to the children while ensuring their safety. Sometimes the visits are supervised by a supervisory agency or a trained mental health professional. Other times visits can be supervised by a trusted friend or family member. Visits will typically not be supervised forever. Supervised visits are designed to protect the children while the visiting parent resolves the issues that necessitate supervision in the first place.

Other remedies include, but are not limited to, exchanging the children in a public place, parenting and/or co-parenting classes, anger management, therapy, and prohibitions against the parent drinking alcohol while with the children.

The judge or custody evaluator also attempts to select the remedy that protects the children while simultaneously posing the least amount of burden on them.

8.26   My spouse keeps saying he'll get custody because there were no witnesses to his abuse and I can't prove it. Is he right?

No. Most domestic violence is not witnessed by others, and judges know this. If you have been a victim of abusive behavior by your spouse, or if you have witnessed your children as victims, your testimony is likely to be the most compelling evidence.

Be sure to tell your attorney about anyone who may have either seen your spouse's behavior or spoken to you or your children right after an abusive incident. They may be important witnesses in your custody case.

8.27   I am concerned about protecting my child from abuse by my spouse. Which types of past abuse by my spouse are important to tell my attorney?

You should give your attorney a full history of the following:

- Hitting, kicking, pushing, shoving, or slapping you or your child
- Sexual abuse
- Threats to harm you or the child
- Threats to abduct your child
- Suicide threats
- Destruction of property
- Alcohol or drug abuse
- Torture of or harm to pets
- Requiring your child to keep secrets

The process of writing down past events may help you to remember other incidents of abuse that you had forgotten. Be as complete as possible.

8.28 **What documents or items should I give my attorney to help prove the history of domestic violence by my spouse?**

The following may be useful exhibits if your case goes to court:

- Photographs of injuries
- Photographs of damaged property
- Abusive or threatening notes, letters, or e-mails
- Abusive or threatening voice or text messages
- Your journal entries about abuse
- Police reports
- Medical records
- Court records
- Criminal and traffic records
- Damaged property, such as torn clothing

These documents and items should, likewise, be provided to the custody expert or guardian *ad litem.* Tell your attorney which of these you have or are able to obtain. Ask your attorney whether others can be acquired through a subpoena or other means.

8.29 **I want to talk to my spouse about our child, but all he or she wants to do is argue. How can I communicate without it always turning into a fight?**

Because conflict is high between you and your spouse, consider the following:

- Ask your attorney to help you obtain a court order for custody and parenting time that is specific and detailed. This lowers the amount of necessary communication between you and your spouse.
- Put as much information in writing as possible.
- Consider using e-mail or text messaging, especially for less urgent communication.
- Consider using Internet resources such as: www.ourfamilywizard.com
- Avoid criticisms of your spouse's parenting.
- Avoid telling your spouse how to parent.

117

- Be factual and business-like.
- Acknowledge to your spouse the good parental qualities he or she displays, such as being concerned, attentive, or generous.
- Keep your child out of any conflicts.

You can only control your behavior. By focusing on you and how you respond to your spouse, conflict with your spouse has the potential to decrease.

8.30 What if the child is not returned from parenting time at the agreed upon time? Should I call the police?

Calling the police should be done only as a last resort if you feel that your child is at risk for abuse or neglect, or if your attorney has advised you that such a call is warranted. The involvement of law enforcement officials in parental conflict can result in far greater trauma to a child than a late return at the end of a parent's time.

The appropriate response to a child being returned late depends upon the circumstances. If the problem is a recurring one, talk to your attorney regarding your options. It may be that a change in the schedule would be in the best interest of your child. Regardless of the behavior of the other parent, make every effort to keep your child out of any conflicts between the adults.

8.31 If I have primary custody, may I move out of state without the permission of the court?

No. A custodial parent must obtain permission of the court prior to moving out of state with a child. If your former spouse agrees to your move, contact your attorney to prepare the necessary documents to be filed with the court. Make sure you protect yourself: if you move without a court order, your spouse may later have a change of heart and allege you left without his/her knowledge or consent. Unless you and your spouse already agreed in a prior court order that you may leave with the children, you will need to get a court order permitting you to move with the children.

If your former spouse objects to your move, you must file a motion seeking an order allowing you to remove the children from the state. The motion should explain all the reasons for the move. It will then be up to the judge to determine whether the move is in the children's best interest. A custody expert or a guardian *ad litem* will usually have to be hired to do an investigation as to whether or not the move is in the children's best interest.

In relocation cases, there are two competing interests: the desire of a parent to leave versus the impact the move will have on the relationship between the noncustodial parent and the child. The stronger the relationship between the child and the noncustodial parent, the more convincing the reasons for the move will need to be. Conversely, if the noncustodial parent rarely sees the child, exhibits little interest in the child, or lives in another state, the court may permit the move for a lesser reason.

8.32 What information should I gather to improve my chances of success if I am seeking to move with the children?

Judges, custody experts, and guardians *ad litem* are interested in the reasons for the move. If, for example, you are requesting the move as a result of job transfer, collect employment records establishing the need to move. Gather information about the school the children will attend, the community in which they will live, the extracurricular and recreational activities available to them, and the other benefits associated with the new location. This information can include documentation of the quality of the school the children will be attending, the school's high graduation rate, and the low crime rate.

Because the judge will be weighing the move against the impact to the noncustodial parent, develop a long-distance time-sharing schedule that provides substantial parenting time for the noncustodial parent and minimizes the travel burden on both the children and the noncustodial parent.

8.33 After the divorce, can I legally take our children out of the state or out of the country during my parenting time?

Although out-of-state travel is not allowed during the divorce proceedings without the knowledge and consent of the other parent, this is not the case once the divorce has been finalized. Ordinarily, either parent may temporarily remove the children from the state or country for a vacation. Before leaving, the traveling parent must provide the other parent with their itinerary and contact information. International travel often requires written consent by the other parent. If you anticipate that your ex-spouse will be uncooperative in giving his/her consent, contact your attorney as soon as possible in order to give your attorney plenty of time so court intervention can be sought if need be.

8.34 If I am not given custody, what rights do I have regarding medical records and medical treatment for my child?

Regardless of which parent has physical custody, state law allows both parents to have access to the medical records of their children and to make emergency medical decisions. Make sure you are listed as a parent with the children's physician in order to access the child's medical records. If you are not listed as the child's parent, doctor's offices will usually add you if you provide a copy of a court order evidencing you are the child's parent.

8.35 If I'm not the primary caregiver, how will I know what's going on at my child's school? What rights to records do I have there?

Regardless of your status as physical custodian, you have a right to have access to your child's school records. Develop a relationship with your child's teachers and the school staff. Request to be put on the school's mailing list for all notices. Find out what is necessary for you to do to get copies of important school information and report cards.

Set aside any acrimony you feel for your ex-spouse. Make a good-faith effort to communicate with the other parent to both share and receive information about your child's progress in school. This will enable you to support your child and each other through any challenging periods of your child's education. It also enables you to share a mutual pride in your child's successes.

Regardless of which parent has physical custody, your child will benefit by your involvement in his/her education through your participation in parent–teacher conferences, attendance at school events, help with school homework, and positive communication with the other parent.

8.36 What if my child does not want to go for his/her parenting time?

One of the most perplexing problems in family court is the child who does not want to go for time-sharing. Parents often raise competing claims. One parent claims the child doesn't want to go with the other parent because the other parent doesn't engage the child, or otherwise mistreats the child. The other parent argues that the custodial parent has alienated the child and negatively influenced the relationship. Sometimes both parents are correct. In considering this dilemma, judges, custody experts, and guardians *ad litem* look to the following:

- What is your child's stated reason for not wanting to go?
- Does your child appear afraid, anxious, or sad?
- Have any legitimate safety issues been disclosed?
- Has there been a history of interference by the custodial parent?
- Does the custodial parent prepare the child for being with the other parent by speaking about the experience with enthusiasm and encouragement?
- Is it possible that the child perceives the custodial parent's anxiety about the situation and is consequently having the same reaction?
- Has the custodial parent consciously or subconsciously subverted the child's transition to the other home by engaging in fun activities with the child just before the pickup?
- Has the noncustodial parent made the parenting time nonthreatening by engaging in activities that the child enjoys rather than making the child do what the parent wants to do or plunking the child down in front of a television for the weekend?

Children deserve to have a relationship with both parents regardless of any hard feelings or mistrust between the parents. Custodial parents need to set aside their anxiety and encourage the children to enjoy time with the other parent. The noncustodial parent must be patient and understand the children's natural aversions to changes to their day-to-day routine. Each child is different and a cooperative approach is best. When both parents work together to address their children's concerns, these issues rarely last. Getting along with the other parent for the sake of your children is also one of the best ways to ensure your child's psychological well-being.

Unfortunately, there are instances where people lose sight of their children's interests as they become overwhelmed by their personal feelings. In these instances, judges, custody experts, and guardians *ad litem* must get involved. Judges treat compliance with court orders for parenting time seriously. If a judge, custody expert, or guardian *ad litem* believes that one parent is intentionally interfering with the other's parenting time or the parent–child relationship, it can not only result in further litigation but ultimately in a loss in custody. With this said, courts want to ensure children are safe. Talk to your attorney about the best approach in your situation.

8.37   What steps can I take to prevent my spouse from getting the children in the event of my death?

Unless the other parent is not fit to have custody, he or she will have first priority as the guardian of your child in the event of your death. Many people have wills naming desired guardians in the event of his/her death. It is helpful to state your preference, but a will does not override a fit parent's right to care for his/her child.

9

Child Support

Whether you will be paying or receiving child support, it is often the subject of much worry. Will you receive enough support to take care of your children? Will you have enough money to live on after you pay your child support? How will you make ends meet?

Most parents want to provide for their children. Today, child-support laws make it possible for parents to have a better understanding of their obligation to support their children. The mechanisms for both payment and receipt of child support are more clearly defined, and help is available for collecting support if it's not paid.

The New Mexico Child Support Guidelines are fairly straightforward and simple, making it easy to calculate child support in most cases.

9.1   What determines whether I will receive child support?

Whether you will receive child support depends upon a number of factors. These include each parent's ability to pay support, how much time your children are living in your household, and what expenses each parent pays on behalf of the children.

If the individual from whom you are attempting to receive support is not the biological or adoptive parent of your child, it is possible you will not receive child support from him or her. Whenever application of the child-support guidelines requires a person to pay more than 40 percent of his/her income for current support, there is a presumption of a substantial hardship justifying a deviation from the guideline amount. In most cases, if an individual is unemployed or underemployed the court will impute minimum wage to that individual and calculate child support as if he/she is earning minimum wage.

9.2 Can I request child support even if I do not meet the six-month residency requirement for a divorce in New Mexico?

Yes. Even though you may not have met the requirements to obtain a divorce, you have a right to seek support for your children. Talk to your attorney or visit the Human Services Department, New Mexico Child Support Division website at: www.hsd.state.nm.us/LookingForAssistance/Child_Support. aspx for contact information and to apply for child-support services.

9.3 Can I get temporary support while waiting for custody to be decided?

A judge has authority to enter a temporary order for custody and child support. This order typically remains in place until a final decree of dissolution of marriage establishing custody is entered. In most cases a hearing for temporary custody and support can be held shortly after the filing of the petition.

9.4 Can I receive temporary support and, if so, how soon can I get it?

Temporary child support is usually paid as part of interim support in divorce cases. Interim support is determined by calculating each party's monthly income and expenses. Any surplus income from either party is equally divided. Once interim support is calculated, the court looks at who is caring primarily for the children and orders the other party to pay those additional amounts to cover the additional costs associated with caring for the children.

Interim support and temporary child support are usually paid from the date the petition for dissolution of marriage is filed and continue until your final decree of dissolution of marriage is entered by the court or until your case is dismissed. As a practical matter, it usually takes a while for interim support to be paid. This is because it takes time to gather and exchange the necessary income and debt documents necessary to calculate interim support and temporary child support. The time frame can be extended even further if the appropriate amount of support cannot be agreed upon between counsel and a hearing needs to be held in order for a determination to be made. In such instances, it is common for the court to order interim support and temporary child support to be paid retroactively for the months no support, or not enough support, was paid. Interim support will not be ordered for any period prior to the filing of the petition for dissolution of marriage. Because there are a number of steps to getting an interim support and temporary child-support order entered, don't delay in discussing your need for support with your attorney.

The following are the common steps in the process:

- You discuss your need for an interim and temporary child support with your attorney.
- A request for the necessary documents is made and interim allocation of income and debts work sheet is prepared.
- An attempt is made to negotiate payment of interim and temporary child support without the need for a hearing.
- Your attorney prepares and files a motion requesting that the court issue an order determining interim and temporary child support. A request for a hearing is filed at the same time.
- A hearing is held.
- The temporary order is signed by the judge and one party is ordered by the court to pay interim and temporary child support.
- Payments begin to be made. If you do not believe your spouse will make these payments voluntarily, it may be possible for an income withholding order to be entered which requires your spouse's employer to withhold support payments directly from your spouse's paycheck. The employer then sends the money to the court-ordered recipient. Some orders direct the employer to send the payments to Child Support Enforcement Division (CSED). If this is the case,

CSED will then send the money to the court-ordered recipient.

If your spouse is not paying you support voluntarily, time is of the essence in obtaining a temporary order for support. This should be one of the first issues you discuss with your attorney.

9.5   How soon does my spouse have to start paying support for the children?

Your spouse may begin paying you support voluntarily at any time but it is common for the court to order that support be paid back to the date of the filing of the petition for dissolution of marriage. A temporary order for support will give you the right to collect the support if your spouse stops paying. Talk to your attorney about court hearings for interim and temporary child support in your county. You may have to wait for up to several months before your temporary hearing can be held.

9.6   How is the amount of child support I'll receive or pay figured?

The New Mexico Child Support Guidelines are governed by statute and set forth the standards by which your child support is calculated. According to the New Mexico Child Support Guidelines, both parents have a duty to contribute to the support of their children in proportion to their respective incomes. As a result, both your income and your spouse's income will factor into the child-support calculation. These guidelines are used whether you have primary physical custody of your children or share time equally (or close to equally).

Other factors the court may consider include:

- The cost of health and dental insurance premiums for the child
- Work-related child-care expenses
- Additional expenses paid on behalf of the children including but not limited to:
    - Extraordinary medical, dental, and counseling expenses (defined as uninsured expenses in excess of $100 per child per year)

- - Any extraordinary educational expenses for the children
  - Transportation and communication expenses for long-distance time-sharing
- Any special educational needs of a child
- The number of children the parties have together
- Court-ordered child support paid to other children (this amount should be subtracted from the payor's gross income)
- Substantial fluctuations in income. If income varies from month to month, the court will use an average of the last twelve months, if available, or last year's income tax return. If income has fluctuated from year to year, it is common for courts to use an average of the last three years' income.
- State and federal assistance may be included as income with the exception of Temporary Assistance for Needy Families (TANF), food stamps, and supplemental security income.

While it is presumed that child support will be paid according to the New Mexico Child Support Guidelines, the parties may agree, or the court may order a higher or lower amount than what the guidelines provide. When a judge orders, or the parties agree to, an amount of support that is different from the New Mexico Child Support Guidelines amount, it is referred to as a *deviation*.

Examples as to when a deviation may be appropriate are:

- Whenever the application of the New Mexico Child Support Guidelines in an individual case would be unjust or inappropriate
- When either parent or child has extraordinary medical costs
- When a child is disabled with special needs
- For juveniles placed in foster care

Every final decree of dissolution of marriage or child-support judgment that deviates from the guideline amount shall contain a statement of the reasons for the deviation. Due to the complexity of calculations under the New Mexico Child Support Guidelines, many attorneys use computer software to calculate child support.

The New Mexico courts have an interactive child-support work sheet available online to help you to calculate your child-support payments. This work sheet can be found at: www.nmcourts.com/cgi/prose_lib/.

9.7   Will the type of custody arrangement or the amount of parenting time I have impact the amount of child support I receive?

As mentioned previously, there are two types of custody in New Mexico: legal custody and physical custody. The presumption in the State of New Mexico is that parties will share joint legal custody of their children. Legal custody speaks to decision making in the major areas of a child's life. These major areas are residence, religion, education, medical, and recreation. Legal custody does not impact child support in and of itself.

Physical custody, or how much time the child spends with each parent, does have an impact on child support. In New Mexico, there are two work sheets on which child support can be calculated. Work sheet A contemplates that there is a primary residential parent who pays for the child's expenses directly while the other parent pays child support to that parent. Work sheet B contemplates that both parents are spending a substantial amount of time with the child and are paying directly for the child's expenses. Work sheet B applies when each parent has the child at least 35 percent of the time. Time is counted using twenty-four-hour periods.

9.8   Is overtime pay considered in the calculation of child support?

Yes. Child support is calculated on each party's gross income. Gross income includes income from any source and includes, but is not limited to, income from salaries, wages, tips, commissions, bonuses, dividends, severance pay, pensions, interest, trust income, annuities, capital gains, Social Security benefits, workers' compensation benefits, unemployment insurance benefits, disability insurance benefits, significant in-kind benefits that reduce personal living expenses, prizes, and alimony or maintenance received.

9.9 What if my spouse is self-employed or receives rental income?

In these instances gross income is defined as gross receipts minus ordinary and necessary expenses required to produce such income. Ordinary and necessary expenses do not include expenses determined by the court to be inappropriate for purposes of calculating child support.

9.10 My spouse has a college degree but refuses to get a job. Will the court consider this in determining the amount of child support?

Yes. Income means actual gross income of a parent if employed to full capacity or potential income if unemployed or underemployed. Therefore, the earning capacity of your spouse or you may be considered instead of current income. The court can look at your or your spouse's work history, education, skills, health, and job opportunities.

Income need not be imputed to the primary custodial parent actively caring for a child of the parties who is younger than the age of six or disabled.

9.11 Will I get the child support directly from my spouse or from the state?

New Mexico law, Section 40-4A-4.1 NMSA 1978, requires that child support be immediately withheld from the income of the payor of child support, unless there is a good reason not to have the support automatically withheld. Employers routinely withhold child support from employee wages just as they withhold taxes or retirement. Child support will not be withheld without an income withholding order. Child support will, likewise, not be withheld if the parties to the proceeding enter into a written agreement not to withhold income. If the parties enter an agreement to waive wage withholding, the payee has the right to insist upon wage withholding at a future date. Many agreements in which wage withholding is waived include a provision stating that the payor will be subject to wage with-holding if a one-month support delinquency accrues.

If a parent's income is being withheld by his or her em-ployer, the employer withholds the employee's child-support obligation from his/her check and sends the child-support pay-ment to the New Mexico Child Support Enforcement Division (CSED). CSED then sends the child support to the parent re-ceiving support.

If the parents do not wish to have their child support processed through CSED, they can also agree upon an auto-matic monthly bank draft where child support is automatically drafted from the payor's bank account into the recipient's bank account each month.

9.12 What are the pros and cons of having my support pay-ments processed by CSED?

CSED keeps a record of all child-support payments made and therefore has a record of whether child support is current or whether there is delinquency and, if so, in what amount. For this reason, CSED protects both parents. Payments may, how-ever, be processed more slowly than payments paid directly between parents.

If you are the payor of child support, it is always impor-tant to have a record of any amounts paid. For this reason, child support should never be paid in cash as it is difficult, if not impossible, to prove that these payments were made.

9.13 How soon can I expect my child-support payments to start arriving?

A number of factors may affect the date on which you will begin receiving your child support. Here are the usual steps in the process:

- A child-support amount and start date for the support are decided either by agreement between you and your spouse or by the judge.
- Either your attorney or your spouse's attorney pre-pares the court order.
- The attorney who did not write the court order re-views and approves it.

- The court order is taken to the judge for signature.
- An income withholding order is drafted, filed, and delivered to the payor's employer, asking that child support be withheld from future paychecks.
- Your spouse's employer withholds the support from the paycheck.
- The child support is sent by the employer to CSED.
- CSED sends the money to you, either by direct deposit or mail.

As you can see, there are a lot of steps in this process. Plan your budget knowing that the initial payment of child support might be delayed.

9.14 Will some amount of child support be withheld from every paycheck?

If child support is paid via an income withholding order, monthly support is usually divided by the number of checks the employer receives each year. For example: If an employer issues paychecks twice a month, half of the support will be withheld from each check. If an employer issues weekly checks, the payor's annual support obligation will be determined and divided by fifty-two, the number of checks received by an individual who is paid once a week.

9.15 If my spouse has income other than from an employer, is it still possible to get a court order to withhold my child support from his income?

Yes. Child support can be automatically withheld from most sources of income. These may include unemployment, worker's compensation, retirement plans, and investment income.

9.16 The person I am divorcing is not the biological parent of my child. Can I still collect child support from my spouse?

Unless your spouse has legally adopted your child, it is unlikely. Discuss the facts of your case in detail with your attorney. When you are clear about what will be in the best interest of your child, your attorney can support you in developing a strategy for your case which takes into consideration not only child support but also the future relationship of your spouse with your child.

9.17 Can child support be collected from both the biological parent and the adoptive parent of my child?

When your child was adopted, the biological parent's duty to support your child ended. However, it may be possible for you to collect past-due child support for the period of time before the adoption.

9.18 What happens with child support when our children go to the other parent's home for summer vacation? Is child support still due?

It depends. Whether child support is adjusted during extended parenting times with the noncustodial parent usually depends upon whether child support was calculated based on a Work sheet A or a Work sheet B. Child support calculated using a Work sheet B factors in the amount of time the children spend with each parent on an annual basis and therefore child support typically does not abate during the period of time the children are with the noncustodial parent.

When child support is calculated using a Work sheet A, the court may provide for partial abatement of child support for visitations of one month or longer.

Before your final decree of dissolution of marriage is entered by the court, talk with your attorney about child-support abatement if you are anticipating that the parent paying support will have the child for an extended period.

9.19 What is a *child-support hearing officer*?

Child-support hearing officers are attorneys who are employed by the court to hold hearings regarding child-support matters. At the conclusion of these hearings, the child-support hearing officer prepares and files a report with the clerk of the court. Within ten days after being served with notice of the filing of the report, either party may file written objections which will be heard by a district court judge.

9.20   After the divorce, if I choose to live with my new partner rather than marry, can I still collect child support?

Yes. Although spousal support may end if you live with your partner, child support does not terminate for this reason.

9.21   Can I still collect child support if I move to another state?

Yes. A move out of state will not end your right to receive child support. However, the amount of child support could be changed if other circumstances change, such as income or costs for exercising parenting time.

9.22   Can I expect to continue to receive child support if I remarry?

Yes. Your child support will continue even if you remarry.

9.23   How long can I expect to receive child support?

Under New Mexico law, child support is ordinarily ordered to be paid until the child is both eighteen and graduated from high school. Child support terminates at the age of nineteen whether the child has graduated from high school or not. Child support also terminates if the child dies or is emancipated. A child becomes emancipated if he/she is sixteen years of age or older and has entered into a valid marriage, is on active duty with the Armed Forces, or has received a declaration of emancipation from the court.

There are some instances where parents are ordered to pay child support for a longer period of time. If a child is disabled, the court can order the parents to pay child support beyond the age of nineteen. Likewise, if the parties enter into a contract to pay for the child's college expenses, child support can then be paid after the child reaches the age of nineteen. Although the court cannot order a party to pay college expenses, it can enforce an agreement for these expenses to be paid if the parties enter into a contract agreeing to pay their child's post-majority expenses.

9.24   Does interest accrue on past-due child support?

Yes. Interest accrues on delinquent child-support payments at a rate of 4 percent.

9.25   What can I do if my former spouse refuses to pay child support?

If your former spouse is not paying child support, you may take action to enforce the court order either with the help of your attorney or the assistance of a child-support attorney. Unlike a private attorney, you do not pay for the services of a child-support attorney. The website for the New Mexico Child Support Enforcement Division (CSED) is: www.hsd.state. nm.us/Child_Support_Enforcement_Division.aspx. The judge may order payment of both the current amount of support and an additional amount to be paid each month until the past-due child support (referred to as *arrearages*) is paid in full.

You may request that your former spouse's state and federal tax refunds be intercepted and paid toward the child-support arrearage. It may also be possible to garnish the non-paying parent's wages or have their property seized and sold.

Driver's licenses or professional licenses may also be suspended if a parent falls behind on child-support payments. However, if there is a payment plan for the payment of arrearages, then licenses will not be suspended. If a parent is behind on their child-support obligation by $2,500 or more, the individual's application for a passport can be denied.

Your former spouse may also be found in contempt of court if the failure to pay support is intentional. Possible consequences include being fined or jailed and having to pay the attorney's fees of the individual seeking enforcement.

These things do not happen automatically. The individual who is owed support must alert CSED and/or the court of the payor's nonpayment of child support.

9.26   I live outside New Mexico. Will the money I spend on airline tickets to see my children impact my child support?

The New Mexico Child Support Guidelines allows transportation and communication expenses necessary for long-distance visitation or time-sharing to be included in the calculation of child support.

9.27   Are expenses such as work-related child care supposed to be taken out of my child support?

The New Mexico Child Support Guidelines provides that each parent pay a percentage of the work- or school-related child-care expenses. These expenses can be included in the calculation of child support or paid according to the percentages of income earned by each party.

9.28   How does providing health insurance for my child affect my child-support amount?

If you pay the health insurance premium for your child, the amount you pay will be taken into account when calculating child support. You will receive a credit for the amount you pay per month for your child's health insurance premium.

9.29   Am I required to pay for my child's uninsured medical expenses from the child support I receive?

Your child-support order should spell out how uninsured medical expenses will be paid. The court usually orders that these expenses be paid according to the percentages of income earned by each party.

9.30   What is a *cash medical support order*?

The *Mandatory Medical Support Act* requires parents to provide or purchase health insurance coverage for their minor children when such coverage is available. If the court finds that health insurance coverage for the child is not available to the parent through an employment-related or other group health care insurance plan, the court requires the parent to pay cash in a specific dollar amount. This is referred to as a *cash medical support order*.

Cash medical support is an amount paid in a child-support order toward the cost of health care provided by a public entity, such as Medicaid. For example, if your child is on Medicaid, the noncustodial parent may be required to pay a monthly amount in cash medical support to reimburse Medicaid for expenses paid on your child's behalf.

9.31 Am I required to pay for the general, everyday expenses for my child with the child support I receive?

Yes, if you are receiving child support, under the New Mexico Child Support Guidelines, you are responsible for expenses for your child such as housing, clothing, food, haircuts, and school lunches. The exceptions to this are uninsured medical expenses and recreational activities, which are commonly shared according to the percentages of income earned by each party.

9.32 Do I have to prove how child support was used?

The recipient of child support is not required to keep receipts or account for how child support is spent.

9.33 If I am the payor of child support, can I reduce my child-support payment when I purchase things for my children?

No. Child support can be modified only by court order.

9.34 Can my spouse be required by the final decree of dissolution of marriage to pay for our child's private elementary and high school education?

Maybe. If the children attended private school during the marriage, it is conceivable that the court would order that the children continue to attend private school. The way in which tuition will be paid will have to be determined based on the relative incomes of each of the parents. If you want your spouse to share this expense for your children, talk it over with your attorney. Be sure to provide your attorney with information regarding tuition, fees, and other expenses related to private education.

9.35 Can my spouse be required by the final decree of dissolution of marriage to contribute financially to our child's college education?

The legal duty of a parent to support a child does not include payment for college education. However, if your spouse agrees to pay this expense, it can be included in the final decree of dissolution of marriage and it will be an enforceable court order. Such a provision is ordinarily included in a divorce decree only as a result of a negotiated settlement.

If your decree includes a provision for payment of college education expenses, be sure it is specific. Terms to consider include:

- What expenses are included? For example, tuition, room and board, books, fees, travel, and so on.
- Is there a limit? For example, up to the level of the cost of attendance at University of New Mexico or a certain dollar amount.
- When is the payment due?
- For what period of time does it continue?
- Are there any limits on the type of education that will be paid for?

The greater the clarity in such a provision, the lower the risk is for misunderstanding or conflict years later.

9.36 Can child support be modified after an order is entered?

Child support can be modified when there is a material and substantial change in circumstances. There is a presumption of a material and substantial change in circumstances if application of the New Mexico Child Support Guidelines would result in a deviation upwards or downwards of more than 20 percent of the existing child-support obligation. Also, if the petition for modification is filed more than one year after the filing of the previous child-support order, there is a presumption that there has been a material and substantial change of circumstances.

If you agree to a child-support modification, you must file an order with the court that memorializes the new child support to be paid. If an order is not filed with the court, the court will hold the child-support payor to the amount reflected in the most recent child-support order filed with the court.

9.37 How do I know if child support should be modified?

All child-support orders must contain a provision for the annual exchange of financial information upon a written request by either party. The financial information to be furnished shall include:

- Federal and state tax returns, including all schedules, for the year preceding the request
- W-2 statements for the year preceding the request
- Internal Revenue Service Form 1099s for the year preceding the request
- Work-related day care statements for the year preceding the request
- Dependent medical insurance premiums for the year preceding the request
- Wage and payroll statements for four months preceding the request

If, after exchanging this information, it appears that a material and substantial change in circumstances has occurred, then it would appear that child support should be modified.

10

Spousal Support

The mere mention of the words alimony or spousal support might stir your emotions and start your stomach churning. If your spouse has filed for divorce and is seeking alimony, you might see it as a double injustice—your marriage is ending and you feel like you have to pay for it, too. If you are seeking spousal support, you might feel hurt and confused that your spouse is resistant to helping support you, even though you may have interrupted your career to stay home to care for your children. Alimony is one of the most emotional and difficult issues in a divorce. Also, unlike child support, it is quite subjective in New Mexico and does not rely primarily on a mathematical calculation. Thus, judges, and certainly different judicial districts, may treat this issue differently.

Learning more about New Mexico's laws on *spousal support,* also referred to as *alimony* or *maintenance,* can help you move from your emotional reaction to the reality of possible outcomes in your case. Uncertainty about the precise amount of alimony that may be awarded or the number of years it might be paid is not unusual. Work closely with your attorney. Be open to possibilities. Try looking at it from your spouse's perspective. Alimony is not supposed to punish the payor, but rather is designed to provide a more equal financial footing to both parties postdivorce.

With the help of your attorney, you will know the best course of action to take toward an alimony decision you can live with after your divorce is over.

10.1 Are there different types of spousal support in New Mexico?

Yes. In New Mexico, a court can award spousal support for a fixed or indefinite period to be paid in a one-time lump-sum payment or in a single sum to be paid in installments. In addition, an award of spousal support can be labeled as modifiable or nonmodifiable, which indicates whether it is intended that the award can be changed (made greater or smaller, or for a shorter or longer period of time) after the divorce decree is entered. In addition to the type of payments and the modifiability, spousal support can be categorized by the purpose of the support and the need of the receiver of support.

Rehabilitative spousal support is designed to provide the receiving spouse with education, training, work experience, or other forms of rehabilitation that increases the receiving spouse's ability to earn income and become self-supporting. The court may even include a specific rehabilitation plan with the award of rehabilitative spousal support and may condition the ongoing payment of support upon compliance with that plan. This is generally thought of as the type of support that helps a spouse to get back on his/her feet.

Transitional spousal support is supposed to supplement the income of the receiving spouse for a limited period of time, which should be clearly set out in the order of support. Generally, this type of support is awarded when a spouse has been working part-time but is moving into a full-time position or in the event of a life transition such as becoming eligible to receive Social Security income.

Permanent spousal support is generally support that is paid for an indefinite duration and is usually awarded in those cases of long-term, traditional marriages where there is a large disparity in income and there is an inability for a spouse to rehabilitate themselves into being self-supporting. In New Mexico, a court retains jurisdiction to modify periodic spousal support when the parties have been married more than twenty years, unless the parties specifically agree that no spousal support shall be awarded or that the court shall not retain jurisdiction to modify the support award. Thus, "permanent" in this case generally means that a court may keep oversight of the case and schedule a review hearing if the circumstances of either party change, such as retirement or a health concern.

10.2 How will I know if I am eligible to receive spousal support?

Talk with your attorney about whether or not you are a candidate for spousal support. Unfortunately, the opinions of New Mexico judges about awarding spousal support vary greatly. Among the factors that may affect your eligibility to receive spousal support are:

- The age, health, and the means of support for both spouses
- The current and future earnings and the earning capacity of the respective spouses
- The good-faith efforts of the respective spouses to maintain employment or to become self-supporting
- The reasonable needs of the respective spouses, including:
  - The standard of living of the respective spouses during the term of the marriage
  - The maintenance of medical insurance for the respective spouses
  - The appropriateness of life insurance, including its availability and cost, to secure payments after the payor's death
- The duration of the marriage
- The amount of property awarded or confirmed to the respective spouses
- The type and nature of the respective spouses' assets
- Income produced by property owned by the respective spouses
- Agreements entered into by the spouses in contemplation of the dissolution of marriage
- Your contributions to the marriage, including interruption of your career for the care of children or to support your spouse's career

Every case for spousal support is unique. Providing your attorney with clear and detailed information about the facts of your marriage and current situation will allow him/her to make an alimony assessment in your case.

10.3 If I did not want the divorce, why do I need to pay the other party spousal support?

Although it may not feel fair, New Mexico does not consider which party wants the divorce or if one party was at fault in causing the breakdown of the marriage when determining if an award of spousal support is appropriate.

10.4 What information should I provide to my attorney if I want spousal support?

If your attorney advises you that you may be a candidate for spousal support, be sure to provide complete facts about your situation, including:

- A history of the interruptions in your education or career for the benefit of your spouse, including transfers or moves due to your spouse's employment
- A history of the interruptions in your education or career for raising children, including periods during which you worked part-time
- Your complete educational background, including the dates of your schooling or training and degrees earned
- Your work history, including the names of your employers, the dates of your employment, your duties, your pay, and the reasons you left
- Any pensions or other benefits lost due to the interruption of your career for the benefit of the marriage
- Your health history, including any current diagnoses, treatments, limitations, and medications
- Your monthly living expenses (or postdivorce budget), including anticipated future expenses such as health insurance and tax on alimony
- A complete list of the debts for you and your spouse
- Income for you and your spouse, including all sources

Also include any other facts that might support your need for spousal support, such as other contributions you made to the marriage, upcoming medical treatment, or a lack of available jobs in the field in which you were formerly employed.

No two cases are alike. The better the information your attorney has about your situation, the easier it will be for him or her to assess your case for spousal support.

10.5 How is the amount of alimony calculated?

Unlike child support, there are not specific guidelines in New Mexico for determining the amount of spousal support. A judge will look at the expenses and incomes of you and your spouse, after giving consideration to the payment and receipt of child support.

Judges are given a lot of discretion to make their own decision on spousal support without the benefit of specific guidelines. Consequently, the outcome of a spousal support ruling by a judge can be one of the most unpredictable aspects of your divorce.

10.6 My spouse told me that because I had an affair during the marriage, I have no chance to get spousal support even though I quit my job and have cared for our children for many years. Is it true that I have no case?

That is not the law in New Mexico. Your right to support will be based upon many factors, but having an affair is not an absolute bar to getting spousal support. New Mexico is a no-fault state, so no matter the reason for the divorce, spousal support is to be awarded on economic, not moral, grounds. However, if your affair had a financial impact on the marital estate, it may be taken into consideration when determining an award of spousal support.

10.7 My spouse makes a lot more money than he reports on our tax return, but he hides it. How can I prove my spouse's real income to show he can afford to pay spousal support?

Alert your attorney to your concerns. Your attorney can then take a number of actions to determine your spouse's income with greater accuracy. They are likely to include:

- More thorough discovery
- An examination of check registers and bank deposits
- Review of purchases made by your spouse
- Inquiries about travel
- Depositions of third parties who have knowledge of income or spending by your spouse
- Subpoena of records of places where your spouse has made large purchases or received income
- Comparison of income claimed with expenses paid

Attorneys sometimes hire forensic accountants or other professionals to assist in uncovering true income in such cases. These professionals will look at additional areas for discovery of additional income. In addition, they may do a "lifestyle analysis" to demonstrate that the lifestyle your spouse and/or you enjoyed would only be possible if there were additional unreported sources of income.

By partnering with your attorney, you may be able to build a case to establish your spouse's actual income as greater than is shown on tax returns. If you filed joint tax returns, discuss with your attorney any other implications of erroneous information on those returns.

10.8 I want to be sure the records on the spousal support I pay are accurate, especially for tax purposes. What's the best way to ensure this?

Always pay spousal support, and any other forms of support or payments, to your spouse in a manner that is traceable. This means write a check, get a money order, or wire funds with a printed receipt.

Copies of canceled checks and paid money orders are acceptable to both the IRS and to the court as proof that you made your alimony payments. You certainly do not want to rely on your spouse to keep these records or face your spouse coming back after years and saying the payments were not received. The proof of payments will protect you. These records should be retained for as long as possible, or at least until there is no possibility that any court or agency may wish to see evidence of your payments.

10.9 What effect does spousal support have on my taxes?

Generally, if you are required to pay spousal support pursuant to a court order, your spousal support payments are tax deductible. Likewise, if you receive spousal support pursuant to a court order, you must pay income tax on the amount received. Exceptions to this may be agreed upon by the parties. There are very specific requirements by the IRS to allow a person paying spousal support to deduct those payments from their income and a tax professional and attorney should be consulted before attempting to do so.

10.10 What types of payments are considered spousal support?

Payments to a third party on behalf of your spouse under the terms of your final decree of dissolution of marriage may be treated as payment of spousal support if specifically set out in the final decree. These may include payments for your spouse's medical expenses, housing costs, taxes, and tuition. These payments are treated as if they were received by your spouse then paid to the third party. Additionally, if you pay the premiums on a life insurance policy that is owned by your spouse, those payments may be considered spousal support. Finally, if you are ordered to pay for expenses for a house owned by you and your spouse, some of your payments may be considered spousal support.

10.11 What is the difference between spousal support and division of property?

Spousal support and the division of property serve two distinct purposes. The purpose of alimony is to provide financial support to a spouse. In contrast, the purpose of a property division is to distribute the marital assets equitably between you and your spouse. This is why a court will consider what is received as property division by a spouse when they are receiving spousal support. However, a large award of property, especially if it is not income-producing, does not mean a person will not be eligible for spousal support.

10.12 How long can I expect to receive spousal support?

Like your right to receive spousal support, how long you will receive it will depend upon the facts of your case. In general, the longer your marriage and the greater the disparity in ability to produce income, the stronger your case is for a long-term support award.

You may receive only transitional support or you may receive permanent, modifiable support. Talk to your attorney about the facts of your case to get a clearer picture of the possible outcomes in your situation.

10.13 Does remarriage affect my spousal support award?

Yes. Under New Mexico law, unless your final decree of dissolution of marriage provides otherwise, spousal support ends upon the remarriage of the recipient. The remarriage of the person paying spousal support generally does not affect the spousal support award.

10.14 Does the death of my former spouse affect my spousal support?

Yes. Under New Mexico law, unless your final decree of dissolution of marriage provides otherwise, spousal support terminates upon the death of either party. However, if the court order awarding spousal support provided that payments were to continue after the death of the payor, such as a lump-sum award made in several payments, the estate of the deceased may be obligated for the payments.

10.15 Do I have to keep paying spousal support if my former spouse is now living with a new significant other?

Yes. Do not stop making your spousal support payments if you learn that your spouse has begun residing with someone else. Instead, contact your attorney to seek a modification of the spousal support award. Depending on the circumstances and if your former spouse is sharing expenses with their new significant other, support may be reduced or terminated with a new court order but that must be decided on a case-by-case basis.

10.16 Can I continue to collect spousal support if I move to a different state?

Yes. The duty of your former spouse to follow a court order to pay spousal support does not end simply because you move to another state, unless this is a specific provision in your decree.

10.17 What can I do if my spouse stops paying spousal support?

If your spouse stops paying the support they were ordered to pay you, see your attorney about your options for enforcing your court order. The judge may order the support be taken from a source of your spouse's income or from a financial account belonging to your spouse.

If your spouse is intentionally refusing to pay spousal support, talk to your attorney about whether pursuing a contempt of court action would be effective. In a contempt action, your spouse may be ordered to appear in court and provide evidence explaining why support has not been paid. Possible consequences for contempt of court include a jail sentence or a fine.

10.18 Can I return to court to modify spousal support?

It depends. If your final decree of dissolution of marriage provides that your support order is *nonmodifiable,* then it may not be modified. Also, your final decree may not be modified to award spousal support if spousal alimony was not awarded in the original final decree dissolving the marriage.

If your support order was modifiable and there has been a material change in the circumstances of either you or your spouse, you may seek to have spousal support modified. Some reasons that a modification may be appropriate are if either party had a change in income either through a new job or loss of employment or if either party develops a serious illness that affects their ability to earn income.

A request seeking additional spousal support may not be granted if the time for payment of the spousal support allowed under the original divorce decree has already passed and if all of the required payments were made. If you think you have a basis to modify your spousal support award, contact your attorney at once to be sure a timely modification request is filed with the court.

10.19 My spouse told me that she is going to file for bankruptcy to avoid paying me spousal support. Can she do this?

No. Spousal support payments are considered *domestic support obligations (DSO)*. Under current bankruptcy law, a person cannot avoid paying a DSO by discharging it in a bankruptcy action. The spousal support continues despite a bankruptcy filing.

10.20 In my divorce, I waived spousal support but now I have lost my job and need assistance. Can I go back to court for spousal support?

It is unlikely that a court would award you spousal support if you waived it in your final decree of dissolution of marriage. Once you waive spousal support, you generally waive it forever. The exception to this is if your final decree provided that you could come back to court later to seek support of if you provided in your final decree that the court would maintain jurisdiction to consider an award of spousal support in the future.

11

Division of Property

You never imagined that you would face losing the house you and your spouse so happily moved into—the house where you celebrated family traditions and that you spent countless hours making "home." Your spouse wants it and your lawyer says it might have to be sold.

During a divorce, you will decide whether you or your spouse will take ownership of everything from bathroom towels to the stock portfolio. Suddenly you find yourself having a strong attachment to that lamp in the family room or the painting in the hallway. Why does the coin collection suddenly take on new meaning?

Do your best to reach agreement regarding dividing household goods. Enlist the support of your attorney in deciding which assets should be valued by an expert, such as the family business or real estate. From tax consequences to replacement value, there are many factors to consider in deciding whether to fight to keep an asset, to give it to your spouse, to split it, or to have it sold.

Like all aspects of your divorce, take one step at a time. By starting with the items most easily divided, you and your spouse can avoid paying lawyers to litigate the value of that 1980s album collection.

11.1   What system does New Mexico use for dividing property?

New Mexico is a community property state and the law provides for an equal division of community property and debts acquired during your marriage. The court will make a division that comes as close to a 50-50 division as is practical, but mathematical exactness is not required.

Regardless of how title is held, the court can use its discretion to make a division of the marital assets. The court will usually try to divide the property equally between the parties. Sometimes, if spousal support is owed from one spouse to the other and it makes sense under the circumstances, the court may make an unequal division, allocating some extra portion of property to the spouse who needs financial support. Otherwise, much like a civil business partnership, each marital partner is entitled to an equal amount of the property that is being divided.

If the property simply cannot be divided even close to equally due to the nature of the property the parties own, the court can require the spouse who receives the larger amount of property to pay an *equalization payment* to the other spouse, perhaps in a lump sum or in payments over time, so that the goal of an equal division can be obtained.

11.2   What does *community property* mean, and when does the "community" begin and end?

Community property is a term used in nine states, including New Mexico, under which each spouse holds a one-half interest in property that was acquired during the marriage from the physical labor or earnings of either spouse. Community property will be things like merchandise that is purchased from the wages earned by either spouse, or it can be the sculpture that one spouse created with his hands. It is a system that was brought to this country by the Spanish explorers who populated the early Western states, and has remained in place since the early days of the country.

Under New Mexico law, virtually all property acquired during the marriage by either spouse belongs to both spouses, regardless of who earned it or in whose name it is titled. Exceptions include gifts, inherited property, property agreed to be separate property between spouses, or an award for certain personal injury damages, which is further discussed below as separate property.

In New Mexico, the "community" begins upon marriage, and continues until the day of divorce. Unlike other states that end the "community estate" upon the spouses physically separating from each other or upon the filing for divorce, the community in New Mexico normally ends upon the filing of a final decree of divorce or upon the death of either spouse. That means that any property acquired and (usually) any debt incurred by either party during the marriage (even while the divorce is pending, which may continue for months or years) constitutes community property and community debt unless a specific court order is obtained saying otherwise.

A temporary order dividing community income and expenses often provides that property acquired and debt incurred after the entry of the temporary order will be presumed to be the separate property or debt of the spouse acquiring such property or incurring such debt. There are often good reasons to enter into this type of order but sometimes there are better reasons not to do so. It is crucial to consult with an attorney about whether to agree to a temporary order because your rights as a spouse may be significantly affected by such an order.

The laws regarding community property differ among the nine states that are "community property states." Make sure you speak to your attorney about how community property is dealt with in New Mexico before making important decisions or agreements.

11.3　How is it determined who gets the house?

The first issue regarding the family home is often a determination of who will retain possession of it while the divorce is pending. Later, it must be decided whether the house will be sold or whether it will be awarded to you or your spouse.

If you and your spouse are unable to reach agreement regarding the house, the judge will decide who keeps it or whether it will be sold and the proceeds distributed between the parties.

If either party keeps the house, the equity in that property will be used as an offset to other community property to be divided. If you want to keep the house you need to decide if you can afford to maintain the property and are willing to give your spouse cash or other property (assets) worth half the equity in the home.

11.4 Should I sell the house during the divorce proceedings?

Selling your home is a big decision. To help you decide what is right for you, ask yourself these questions:

- What will be the impact on my children if the home is sold?
- Can I afford to stay in the house and keep up its payments and expenses after the divorce?
- After the divorce, will I be willing to give the house and yard the time, money, and physical energy required for its maintenance?
- Is it necessary for me to sell the house to pay a share of the equity to my spouse, or are there other options, such as a refinance?
- Would my life be easier if I were in a smaller or simpler home?
- Would I prefer to move closer to the support of friends and family?
- What is the state of the housing market in my community?
- What are the benefits of remaining in this house?
- Can I retain the existing mortgage or will I have to refinance?
- Will I have a higher or lower interest rate (and payments) if I sell the house?
- Can I see myself living in a different home?
- Will I have the means to acquire another home?
- If I don't retain the home and my spouse asks for it, what effect will this have on my custody case?
- Will my spouse agree to the sale of the house?

- What will be the real estate commission and other expenses of sale?
- What will be the costs of preparing the house for sale?
- Can I afford to give up other community property in exchange for the equity in the home?

Selling a home is more than just a legal or financial decision. When deciding whether to sell your home, consider what is important to you in creating your life after divorce. In any event, moving forward with a sale during a divorce usually will require agreement of your spouse, or an order of the court.

11.5 What is meant by *equity* in my home?

Regardless of who is awarded your house, the court will need to balance the *equity* in the house between the parties. Equity means the difference between the value of the home and the amount owed in mortgages against the property.

For example, if the first mortgage is $50,000 and the second mortgage from a home equity loan is $10,000, the total debt owed against the house is $60,000. If your home is valued at $100,000, the equity in your home is $40,000 ($100,000 value minus $60,000 in mortgages equals $40,000 equity.)

If one of the parties remains in the home, the issue of how to give the other party his or her share of the equity must be considered. From the example above, if the home is community property, the spouse who retains the house will owe the other spouse $20,000. This can be paid by that spouse receiving $20,000 of value from other assets (such as the entirety of a $20,000 savings account), or the spouse who keeps the house can pay the $20,000 by taking out a loan or by paying monthly payments plus interest to the other spouse.

11.6 How will the equity in our house be divided?

There are two questions here—whether the equity will be equally divided, and how, exactly, the money is obtained and distributed.

If all the money that went into the house—the down payment and the monthly payments—was money earned during marriage, the equity will probably be equally divided.

If one of you owned the house before marriage but made payments with community property during the marriage, the equity may be partly community and partly separate property. There has been a case in New Mexico where the Supreme Court created a formula to determine how to divide the equity in a home in such circumstances. You should discuss any such facts with your lawyer and make sure the lawyer is fully aware of all sources of money that have been invested in the purchase or pay down of any mortgage on the house.

As to the "mechanics" of distributing the equity, if your home is going to be sold, the equity in the home will most likely be divided at the time of the closing of the sale, after the costs of the sale have been paid.

If either you or your spouse will be awarded the house, there are a number of options for the other party being compensated for his or her share of the equity in the marital home. These could include:

- The spouse who does not receive the house receives other community assets to compensate for the value of the equity.
- The person who remains in the home agrees to refinance the home, immediately or at some future date, and to pay the other party his or her share of the equity.
- The parties agree that the property be sold at a future date, or upon the happening of a certain event such as the youngest child completing high school or the remarriage of the party keeping the home.

As the residence is often among the most valuable assets considered in a divorce, it is important that you and your attorney discuss the details of its disposition. These include:

- Valuation of the property
- Refinancing to remove a party from liability for the mortgage
- The dates on which certain actions should be taken, such as listing the home for sale
- The real estate agent
- Costs for preparing the home for sale
- Making mortgage payments

If you and your spouse do not agree regarding which of you will remain in the home and the related terms for division of the equity, the court will decide who keeps it or may order the property sold.

11.7   Who keeps all the household goods until the decree is signed, and after divorce?

The court will ordinarily not make any decisions about who keeps the household goods on a temporary basis, unless the parties force the court to consider the question. Most couples attempt to resolve these issues on their own rather than incur legal fees to dispute them. Remember, it can cost a lot more than those pots and pans are worth to have attorneys battle out who gets to keep them.

If the parties can't decide who is to get what household items, there are multiple ways to deal with the issue. They may utilize the "A/B" list method for distribution. One of the parties makes two lists labeled "A" and "B." Every household item is listed on one of these two lists. The party responsible for making this list should be as careful as possible to try to make the lists as equal in value as possible. Once the two lists are created, the other party gets to pick which list he or she wants, leaving the items on the other list to the party who created the list. Sometimes this is called the "you cut, I pick" method.

Alternatively, where there are multiple items of similar values, the parties can alternate picking them until they are distributed; sometimes, collections (art, coins, stamps, etc.) are divided this way when parties cannot decide who should keep them.

In some cases, an appraiser is hired to put a value on all such items, and the parties (or the court) divide them by value. This is perhaps the most expensive way of dealing with household goods and is rarely warranted.

11.8   How are assets such as cars, boats, and furniture divided, and when does this happen?

In most cases, spouses are able to reach their own agreements about how to divide personal property, such as household furnishings and vehicles.

If you and your spouse disagree about how to divide certain items, it can be wise to consider which are truly valuable to you, financially or otherwise. Perhaps some of the items can be easily replaced. Always consider whether it is a good use of your attorney's fees to argue over items of personal property.

All higher-value items—such as cars and boats—are valued and placed on a spreadsheet so that the "value" is equalized between the parties. Remember, New Mexico is an equal-distribution state and if one party receives an abundance of the "things" from the marriage, the other spouse will usually get an offset in other assets such as cash.

If a negotiated settlement cannot be reached, the issue of the division of your property will be made by the judge at trial.

11.9 What is meant by a *community property and liabilities schedule* and how detailed should mine be?

A *community property and liabilities schedule* is a listing of all property you own and all debts you owe. It may also include a brief description of the property. New Mexico is a mandatory-disclosure state. In other words, New Mexico procedural rules require both parties to a domestic relations action to disclose to the other party relevant information concerning characterization of property (whether community or separate), valuation, division, or distribution of assets or liabilities in a disclosure statement within forty-five days after service of the petition for dissolution of marriage. This disclosure needs to be very detailed to ensure an equal and accurate distribution.

Discuss with your attorney how to proceed in this task. You should note that it will be important to get this inventory done early on in your divorce action, so don't delay speaking to your attorney about what you should be doing to prepare for the initial disclosures on property.

Factors to consider when creating your inventory may include:

- The extent to which you anticipate you and your spouse will disagree regarding the division of your property
- Whether you anticipate a dispute regarding the value of the property either you or your spouse is retaining

- Whether you will have continued access to the property if a later inventory is needed or whether your spouse will retain control of the property
- Whether you or your spouse are likely to disagree about which items are premarital, inherited, or gifts from someone other than your spouse

As part of this community property and liabilities schedule, your attorney may request that you prepare a list of the property that you and your spouse have already divided or a list of the items you want but your spouse has not agreed to give to you.

If you do not have continued access to your property, talk to your attorney about taking photographs or obtaining access to the property to complete your schedule.

11.10 How and when are liquid assets such as bank accounts and stocks divided?

Talk with your attorney early in your case about the temporary domestic order (TDO). In New Mexico, because the community property estate continues while the divorce is pending, all income earned and all debts incurred remain community income and debts. To prevent abuse of one spouse retaining all the community income to which both spouses are entitled or the abuse of one spouse incurring debt the other spouse will also be responsible for, the court issues a temporary domestic order.

Such a TDO prohibits both parties from dissipating assets or incurring debt, other than in the usual course of business and for the necessities of life. Either party may also require that the court enter an interim order, which requires both spouses to first apply all community income to pay all recurring community expenses, such as the mortgage on the marital residence, rent for housing for the spouse not living in the marital residence, utilities, insurances, and all contractual debt the parties will continue to owe, such as car payments, and so on. After all of the recurring expenses are paid, the spouses will then divide the remaining income, with a percentage of such remaining income to be transferred to the party maintaining primary physical custody of the children, if any.

This may include a provision for savings to be drawn upon to pay certain necessary expenses, including payment of attorney's fees. It is not wise for either spouse to engage in "self-help" such as depleting savings or investment accounts without the prior knowledge and agreement from the other spouse. Seeking an interim order requiring the parties to allocate community income and expenses on a temporary basis reduces the risk that your spouse will transfer money out of financial accounts or transfer other assets, or that you will be accused of wrongfully doing so, and it helps to ensure that the community expenses are paid on a regular and responsible basis.

In some cases, couples will agree to divide bank accounts equally at the outset of the case. However, this may not be advisable in your case. Discuss with your attorney what your regular recurring monthly expenses are and assist the attorney with preparing your interim expenses affidavit. Always discuss with your attorney whether you should withdraw any funds or if you should keep an accounting of how you spend money or funds from a bank account once your divorce is in progress.

Stocks are ordinarily a part of the final agreement for the division of property and debts. If you and your spouse cannot agree on how your investments should be divided, the judge will make the decision at trial.

11.11 How is pet custody determined?

Pet custody is determined on a case-by-case basis. New Mexico law is not well established on the matter of pet custody, and most judges appear to be of the opinion that pets are items of property to be divided between the parties like all other assets, rather than being treated like children as to whom the parties may both have rights and obligations after divorce. There is some indication, however, that this attitude, both in society generally and in the courts, may be changing. Factors that other courts have considered include:

- Who held title to the pet?
- Who provided care for the pet?
- Who will best be able to meet the pet's needs?

- Has either party ever abused the pet or shown a propensity for such abuse?
- Some courts have awarded the pet to one party and given the other party certain rights, such as:
  - Specific periods of time to spend with the pet
  - The right to care for the pet when the other person is not able to
  - The right to be informed of the pet's health condition

If it is important to you to be awarded one of your family pets, discuss the matter with your attorney, and find out the current state of the law on the subject. It may be possible to reach a pet care agreement with your spouse that will allow you to share possession of and responsibility for your pets.

However, in New Mexico, at least for now, pets are property and you should presume that they are to be distributed the same way as all other property, with their value or potential liability as an offset against other assets or liabilities.

11.12 How will our property in another state be divided?

Once the New Mexico court has jurisdiction over you and your spouse, it can issue orders concerning the ownership or sale of all property owned by the community no matter where it is located.

For the purposes of dividing your assets, out-of-state property is generally treated the same as property in New Mexico according to the New Mexico *quasi-community property statute*. This law basically says that all real or personal property, except certain separate property, that was acquired by either spouse while domiciled outside New Mexico which would have been community property if the acquiring spouse had been domiciled in New Mexico at the time of the property's acquisition, will be treated as community property. For quasi-community property to be treated as community property, each spouse must be a domiciliary of New Mexico at the time of the dissolution or legal separation. If there is any such property, make sure you explain to your lawyer when, where, and how that property was acquired.

Although a New Mexico court cannot actually change title to property located in another state, a judge can order your spouse to sign a deed or other document to transfer title to you. Procedures in the other state may then be required to actually accomplish the division, sale, or transfer of that real property located outside New Mexico.

11.13 I worked very hard for years to support my family while my spouse completed an advanced degree. Do I have a right to any of my spouse's future earnings?

Your contributions during the marriage are a factor to be considered in both the division of the property and debts, and any award of alimony. Be sure to give your attorney a complete history of your contributions to the marriage and ask about their impact on the outcome of your case.

11.14 Are all of the assets—such as property, bank accounts, and inheritances—that I had prior to my marriage still going to be mine after the divorce?

For the most part, yes. The presumption in New Mexico is that any property that was owned strictly by one party before the marriage, or which was given to just one of the spouses as a gift or an inheritance, remains that spouse's sole and separate property upon divorce. In most cases the court will allow a party to retain an asset brought into the marriage, but there are questions the court will consider in making its determination such as:

- Can the premarital asset be clearly traced? For example, if you continue to own a vehicle that you brought into the marriage, it is likely that it will be awarded to you. However, if you brought a vehicle into the marriage, sold it during the marriage, and spent the proceeds on other property that was used by the community, it is less likely that the court will consider awarding you its value.

- Did you keep the property separate and titled in your name, or did you commingle it with marital assets? Premarital assets you kept separate are more likely to be awarded to you.

160

- Did the other spouse (or community property income) contribute to an increase in the value of the premarital asset, and can the value of that increase be proven? For example, suppose a woman owned a home prior to her marriage. After the marriage, the parties live in the home, continuing to make mortgage payments and improvements to the home. At the time of the divorce, the other spouse seeks a portion of the equity in the home. New Mexico case law contains directions to a trial court for how to consider the value of the home at the time of the marriage, any contributions to the increase in equity made during the marriage, and the evidence of the value of those contributions.

11.15 Will I get to keep my engagement ring?

The short answer is yes. New Mexico considers your engagement ring to be a conditional gift. In other words, if you were given the ring in anticipation of getting married, and you got married, you have fulfilled the condition and it became your ring as your sole and separate property.

11.16 Can I keep gifts and inheritances I received during the marriage?

Gifts and inheritances received during the marriage and premarital assets are considered separate property. Normally, all separate property owned by a party remains the property of that person after divorce. Any gifts from one spouse to the other (or from some other person) are the sole and separate property of the person receiving it. Separate property does not "count" when dividing community property. It belongs to the person who owns it and does not appear on the community property and liabilities schedule of property to be divided.

Any inheritance that you receive—as long as you keep it in an account titled in your name alone—will also be treated as your sole and separate property. If the funds were "commingled" —that is, combined with community property funds—the burden may be on you to trace the separate property funds (that is, show how they came from a separate property source) to the satisfaction of the court in order to retain them as your separate property. The rules for tracing are technical.

There are a number of considerations when using sole and separate funds, such as an inheritance, for community purposes that may affect its treatment at divorce. Make sure you discuss this in detail with your attorney to protect and understand your rights.

11.17   If my spouse and I can't decide who gets what, who decides? Can that person's decision be contested?

If you and your spouse cannot agree on the division of your property, the judge will make the determination after considering the evidence at your trial. If either party is dissatisfied with the decision reached by the judge, an appeal to a higher court is possible.

11.18   What is a *property* or *marital settlement agreement*?

A *property settlement agreement* is a written document that includes all of the financial agreements you and your spouse have reached in your divorce. This may include the division of property, debts, child support, alimony, insurance, tax payment agreements, and agreements for payment of attorney's fees. The agreement may include every issue, or the parties may resolve only some of the issues in the case, and leave others to be determined by the judge, resulting in a *partial marital settlement agreement.*

The property settlement agreement may be a separate document, or it may be incorporated into the decree of divorce, which is the final court order dissolving your marriage.

11.19   How are the values of property determined?

The value of some assets, like bank accounts, is usually not disputed. The value of other assets, such as homes, businesses, or personal property, is more likely to be contested.

If your case proceeds to trial, you may give your opinion of the value of property you own. You or your spouse may also have certain property appraised by an expert. In such cases it may be necessary to have the appraiser appear at trial to give testimony regarding the appraisal and the value of the asset.

If you own substantial assets for which the value is likely to be disputed, talk to your attorney early in your case about the benefits and costs of expert witnesses or other means of establishing values for proof at trial.

11.20 What does *date of valuation* mean?

Because the value of assets can go up or down while a divorce is pending, it can be necessary to determine a set date for valuing the marital assets. This is referred to as the *date of valuation*. You and your spouse may agree on the date the assets should be valued. If you cannot agree, the date of valuation will be the date of trial before the judge. Though it is not always convenient, New Mexico law provides that the valuation date is the closest possible date to that of the divorce trial.

11.21 What happens after my spouse and I approve the property settlement agreement? Do we still have to go to court?

After you and your spouse sign approving the marital or property settlement agreement or the final decree, it must still be approved by the judge. If all issues have been resolved, your documents can be submitted directly to the court for final approval by the judge and entry by the court without the need to appear for a hearing.

Many divorces in New Mexico happen without the parties ever seeing the inside of the courtroom. If you and your spouse can work out all of these details necessary to resolve your case without going to court, the cost of the divorce will be much lower. However, be wary of a "do-it-yourself divorce," which appears cheap. Many of these divorces omit issues or make mistakes of characterization, valuation, or distribution which result in parties spending large amounts of time and money after the divorce has been finalized to fix problems that could have been avoided if the matters had been handled correctly from the beginning. As with most things, it is usually far less expensive to do something right the first time than to try to fix it after the fact.

Also avoid like the plague using a "paralegal service" or "quickie divorce service" to get your divorce. These services, which advertise very cheap rates, have been known to create huge problems—some of which prove to be unfixable. Sometimes, people have lost vast sums of money, or custody of children, without legitimate legal cause. Some of those cases take years to correct. Sometimes the people affected are never able to recover what was lost.

11.22 If my spouse and I think our property settlement agreement is fair, why does the judge have to approve it?

To make sure that your agreement is enforceable, the agreement must be reviewed, approved, and entered by the court. The judge has a duty to ensure that an order relating to child custody appears to serve the best interest of the child. The judge is required to ensure that child support satisfies the statutes governing it, or to make findings showing why an exception is warranted. The court is required to divide community property equally, or set out written findings of a compelling reason to divide it in another way.

A failure to do any of these things could cause the court order to be set aside, provide a basis for appeal, or result in much unnecessary postdivorce litigation.

11.23. What happens to our individual checking and savings accounts during and after the divorce?

Regardless of whose name is on the account, bank accounts are considered community property if the funds in those accounts were acquired during marriage.

Discuss with your attorney the benefits of an interim order to agree on who can use each bank account and for what purpose and the date on which financial accounts should be valued, distributed, converted, or closed.

11.24 Who gets the interest from certificates of deposit, dividends from stock holdings, and so on, during the divorce proceedings?

Generally, in New Mexico, interest is treated as the "rents, issue, and profits," of the underlying property and follows the "character" of the account itself. In other words, if the account itself was a separate property account, the interest is separate property; if it was a community property account, the interest is community property.

Whether you or your spouse receives interest from such assets is decided as a part of the overall division of your property and debts.

11.25 Does each one of our financial accounts have to be divided in half if we agree to an equal division of our assets?

No. Rather than incurring the administrative challenges and expense of dividing each asset in half, you and your spouse can decide that one of you will take certain assets equal to the value of assets taken by the other spouse. This is the balance sheet approach. If necessary, one of you can agree to make a cash payment to the other as an equalization payment or one spouse can take on and pay more of the community debt than the other spouse. Talk to your attorney about various ways to "equalize" the balance sheet.

11.26 What factors determine whether I can get at least half of my spouse's business?

Many factors determine whether you will get a share of your spouse's business and in what form you might receive it. Among the factors the court will look at are:

- Whether your spouse owned the business prior to your marriage
- Whether there was any increase in value of the business during the marriage
- Your role, if any, in operating the business or in increasing its value
- Whether the company "retained earnings" or the owner spouse was fully and fairly compensated with reasonable income during the marriage
- The overall division of the property and debts of the community

If it is determined that the business is entirely or partially community property under New Mexico law, or if the community has a lien on the separate property for inadequate wages paid the community, then both spouses should normally receive half of the value of that community property or lien interest, either as a share of the business asset itself, or as a cash payment for half its value.

If you or your spouse owns a business, it is important that you work with your attorney early in your case to develop a strategy for valuing the business and making your case for how it should be treated in the division of property and debts.

11.27 My husband and I have owned and run our own business together for many years. Can I be forced out of it?

Maybe. Deciding what should happen with a family business when divorce occurs can be a challenge. Because of the risk for future conflict between divorcing spouses, the value of the business is likely to be substantially decreased if both remain owners, but this is not true for all businesses in all cases.

In discussing your options with your lawyer, consider the following questions:

- If one spouse retains ownership of the business, are there enough other assets for the other spouse to receive a fair share of the total marital assets?
- Which spouse has the skills and experience to continue running the business?
- What would you do if you weren't working in the business?
- What is the value of the business?
- What is the market for the business if it were to be sold?
- Could either spouse remain an employee of the business for some period of time even if not an owner?

You and your spouse know your business best. With the help of your lawyers, you may be able to create a settlement that can satisfy you both. If not, the judge will make the decision for you at trial.

11.28 I suspect my spouse is hiding assets, but I can't prove it. How can I protect myself if I discover later that I was right?

First, explore with your lawyer all the ways in which full disclosure might be achieved. If it just is not possible to find and prove everything necessary during the divorce, ask your lawyer to include language in your divorce decree to address your concerns. Insist that it include an acknowledgment by your spouse that the agreement was based upon a full and complete disclosure of your spouse's financial condition, and the consequences if it is later proven that something was omitted. In New Mexico, if it is later discovered that there were property or assets not disclosed, your remedy is to file a civil action for undisclosed and undivided assets. The courts will divide assets if they can be shown to have existed at the time of the divorce pursuant to New Mexico state statute on failure to divide or distribute property upon the entry of a dissolution of marriage or legal separation.

11.29 My spouse says I'm not entitled to a share of his stock options because he gets to keep them only if he stays employed with his company. What are my rights?

Stock options are often very valuable assets. They are also a very complex issue when dividing assets during a divorce for these, among other, reasons:

- Each company has its own rules about awarding and exercising stock options.
- Complete information is needed from the employer.
- There are different methods for calculating the value of stock options, and New Mexico law is fairly undeveloped as to which method should be used.
- The reasons the options were given can impact the valuation. For example, some are given for prior service, some for future performance, some are mixed, and for some there is no evidence either way.
- There are cost and tax considerations when options are exercised.

Rather than being awarded a portion of the stock options themselves, you are likely to receive a share of the sale proceeds when the stock options are exercised.

In New Mexico, stock options are community property to the degree that they are considered—or ruled—to have been "acquired" during the marriage. Generally, they are considered an asset of the community when they are awarded, even if

167

they have not yet vested. However, there are conditions relating to continued, postdivorce employment that may affect the characterization of the stock options as separate property or community property assets, in part or entirely.

If either you or your spouse own stock options, bring that asset to the attention of your lawyer early in your case to allow sufficient time to settle the issues or to be well prepared for trial.

11.30 What is a *prenuptial agreement* and how might it affect the property settlement phase of the divorce?

A *prenuptial agreement,* sometimes referred to as a *premarital* or *antenuptial agreement,* is a contract entered into between two people prior to their marriage. It can include provisions for how assets and debts will be divided in the event the marriage is terminated, as well as terms concerning alimony, although a prenuptial agreement cannot adversely affect a spouse's right to support.

Your property settlement is likely to be greatly impacted by the terms of your prenuptial agreement if the agreement is upheld as valid by the court, because the very purpose of most such documents is to alter how property and debts will be distributed in the event of divorce. *See* Chapter 17 for further information on prenuptial agreements.

11.31. Can a prenuptial agreement be contested during the divorce?

Yes. The court may consider many factors in determining whether to uphold your prenuptial agreement. Among them are:

- Whether your agreement was entered into voluntarily
- Whether your agreement was fair and reasonable at the time it was signed
- Whether you and your spouse gave a complete disclosure of your assets and debts
- Whether you and your spouse each had the opportunity to consult with independent counsel before signing the agreement

- Whether you and your spouse each had enough time to consider the agreement

If you have a prenuptial agreement, bring a copy of it to the initial consultation with your attorney. Be sure to provide your lawyer with a detailed history of the facts and circumstances surrounding reaching and signing the agreement.

11.32 I've heard the old saying, "Possession is nine-tenths of the law." Is that true during divorce proceedings?

Not really. New Mexico is a presumptive equal division community property state and it does not matter which spouse has possession of a community asset when the division of assets is being accomplished.

Consulting with an attorney before the filing of divorce can reduce the risk that assets will be hidden, transferred, or destroyed by your spouse. This is especially important if your spouse has a history of destroying property, frivolous spending, incurring substantial debt, or transferring money without your knowledge.

These are among the possible actions you and your attorney can consider together:

- Placing your family heirlooms or other valuables in a safe location
- Transferring some portion of financial accounts into secure one-party accounts prior to filing for divorce
- Preparing an inventory of the personal property
- Taking photographs or video of the property
- Obtaining copies of important records or statements
- Obtaining a preliminary injunction to prohibit the destruction or damage to property or the withdrawal of funds from accounts and serving the injunction with the petition and summons for divorce

Plans to leave the marital home should also be discussed in detail with your attorney, so that any actions taken early in your case are consistent with your ultimate goals.

Speak candidly with your lawyer about your concerns so a plan can be developed that provides a level of protection that is appropriate to your circumstances.

11.33 I'm Jewish and want my spouse to cooperate with obtaining a *get,* which is a divorce document under our religion. Can I get a court order for this?

Talk to your lawyer about obtaining a *get* cooperation clause in your divorce decree, including a provision regarding who should pay for it. At this time, the law regarding this has not been established in New Mexico, and religious authorities have expressed different views on the validity of a get obtained by direction of the civil courts.

11.34 Who will get the frozen embryo of my egg and my spouse's sperm that we have stored at the health clinic?

The law on this issue is not yet established in New Mexico. The terms of your contract with the clinic may impact the rights you and your spouse have to the embryo, so provide a copy of this contract to your attorney for review.

The potential resolutions include coming to an agreement as to disposition, or giving the power to decide what to do about the embryo to one spouse or the other. If permissible under your contract, you and your spouse may want to consider donating the embryo to another couple.

There are questions as to possible future support obligations for a child, and the law governing "artificial reproduction technology" is in considerable flux. You should discuss the subject with your lawyer and ensure that your lawyer is aware of all current developments in this rapidly changing area of the law.

11.35 Will debts be considered when determining the division of the property?

Yes. The court should consider the marital debts when dividing the property. For example, if you are awarded a car valued at $12,000, but you owe a $10,000 debt on the same vehicle, the court will take that debt into consideration in the overall division of the assets. Similarly, if one spouse agrees to pay substantial marital credit card debt, the obligation will also be considered in the final determination of the division of property and debts.

Division of Property

If your spouse incurred debts that you believe should be his or her sole responsibility, tell your attorney. Some debts may be considered nonmarital or separate debts and treated separately from other debts incurred during the marriage. For example, if your spouse spent large sums of money on gambling or illegal drugs without your knowledge, you may be able to argue that those debts should be the sole responsibility of your spouse.

11.36 What happens to the property distribution if one of us dies before the divorce proceedings are completed?

If your spouse dies prior to your divorce decree being entered, under New Mexico law the case will continue and your personal representative will be substituted into the case in the place of the deceased spouse. This enables the court to make a complete division of the community property and debts and any support issues can be determined. The assets awarded to the deceased spouse in the divorce will become part of their estate. These assets will then be distributed according to their will or according to the laws of the state if they died without a will.

This is obviously a crucial issue and one that should be discussed with your attorney if you think you or your spouse might not survive until the divorce proceedings can be completed.

12

Benefits: Insurance, Retirement, and Pensions

During your marriage, you might have taken certain employment benefits for granted. You might not have given much thought each month to having insurance through your spouse's work. When you find yourself in a divorce, suddenly these benefits come to the forefront of your mind.

You might also, even unconsciously, have seen your own employment retirement benefits as belonging to you and not to your spouse and referred to "my" 401(k) or "my" pension. After all, you are the one who went to work every day to earn it, right?

When you divorce, some benefits arising from your spouse's employment will end, some may continue for a period of time, and others may be divided between you. Retirement funds, in particular, are often one of the most valuable marital assets to be divided in a divorce.

Whether the benefits are from your employer or from your spouse's, with your attorney's help you will develop a better understanding of which benefits the law considers to be "yours," "mine," and "ours" for continuing or dividing.

12.1 Will my children continue to have health coverage through my spouse's work even though we're divorcing?

If either you or your spouse currently provides health insurance for your children, it is very likely that the court will order the insurance to remain in place until your child reaches the age of majority, or for so long as it remains available, and support is being paid for your child.

The cost of insurance for the children will be taken into consideration in determining the amount of child support to be paid.

12.2 Will I continue to have health insurance through my spouse's work after the divorce?

It depends. Investigate the cost of continuing on your spouse's employer-provided plans under the federal law known as *Consolidated Omnibus Budget Reconciliation Act (COBRA)* after the expiration of your previous coverage. This coverage can be maintained for up to three years. However, the cost can be very high, so you will want to determine whether it's a realistic option.

Begin early to investigate your eligibility for coverage on your spouse's health insurance plan after the entry of the final decree of dissolution of marriage and your options for your future health insurance. The cost of your health care is an important factor when pursuing spousal support and planning your postdivorce budget.

12.3 What is a QMSO?

A *QMSO (qualified medical support order)* is a court order providing continued group health insurance coverage for a minor child. A QMSO may also enable a parent to obtain other information about the insurance plan, without having to go through the parent who has the coverage. Rather than allowing only the parent with the insurance to be reimbursed for a claim, under a QMSO, a health insurance plan is required to directly reimburse whoever actually paid the child's medical expense.

12.4 What is a QDRO?

A *QDRO (qualified domestic relations order)* is a court order that requires a retirement or pension plan administrator pay you the share of your former spouse's retirement that was awarded to you in the final decree of dissolution of marriage. In the case of federal retirement plans, this order is called a *COAP (court order acceptable for processing)*. These orders help ensure that a nonemployee spouse receives his/her share directly from the employee spouse's plan.

Obtaining a QDRO or COAP is a critical step in the divorce process. They can be complex documents, and a number of steps are required to reduce future concerns about enforcement and to fully protect your rights. These court orders must comply with numerous technical rules and be approved by the plan administrator, which is often located outside New Mexico.

Whenever possible, court orders dividing retirement plans should be entered at the same time as the final decree of dissolution of marriage.

12.5 How many years must I have been married before I'm eligible to receive a part of my spouse's retirement fund or pension?

Even if your marriage is not of long duration, you may be entitled to a portion of your spouse's retirement fund or pension accumulated during the marriage. For example, if you were married for three years and your spouse contributed $10,000 to a 401(k) plan during the marriage, you would be entitled to one-half of the value of the contribution, and losses or gains, when dividing your property and debts.

12.6 I contributed to my pension plan for ten years before I got married. Will my spouse get half of my entire pension?

Probably not. It is more likely the court will award your spouse only a portion of your retirement that was acquired during the marriage.

If either you or your spouse made premarital contributions to a pension or retirement plan, be sure to let your attorney know. This is information essential to determine which portion of the retirement plan should be treated as separate property, and which portion is community property.

12.7   I plan to keep the same job after my divorce. Will my former spouse get half of the money I contribute to my retirement plan after my divorce?

No. Your former spouse should be entitled to a portion of your retirement accumulated only during the marriage.

Talk with your attorney so that the language of the court order ensures protection of your postdivorce retirement contributions.

12.8   Am I still entitled to a share of my spouse's retirement benefits even though I never contributed to a retirement plan during our twenty-five-year marriage?

Yes. Any monies contributed during the marriage are community property and you are entitled to one-half. Retirements benefits are often the most valuable asset accumulated during a marriage. Consequently, your judge will consider the retirement benefits along with all of the other marital assets and debts when determining a fair division.

12.9   My attorney says I'm entitled to a share of my spouse's retirement benefits. How can I find out how much I get and when I'm eligible to receive it?

More than one factor will determine your rights to collect from your spouse's retirement plan. One factor will be the terms of the court order dividing the retirement benefits. The court order will tell you whether you are entitled to a set dollar amount, a percentage, or a fraction to be determined based upon the length of your marriage and how long your spouse continues to work. For a defined benefit plan, such as a pension, the fraction used by the court to determine how much you are eligible to receive will be the number of years you were married while your spouse was employed at that company divided by the total number of years your spouse is employed with the company.

Another factor will be the terms of the retirement plan itself. Some provide for lump-sum withdrawals; others issue payments in monthly installments. Review the terms of your court order and contact the plan administrator to obtain the clearest understanding of your rights and benefits.

12.10 If I am eligible to receive my spouse's retirement benefits, when am I eligible to begin collecting them? Do I have to be sixty-five to collect them?

It depends upon the terms of your spouse's retirement plan. In some cases it is possible to begin receiving your share at the earliest date your spouse is eligible to receive them, regardless of whether or not he or she elects to do so. Check the terms of your spouse's plan to learn your options.

12.11 What happens if my former spouse is old enough to receive benefits but I'm not?

Ordinarily you will be eligible to begin receiving your share of the benefits when your former spouse begins receiving his/hers. Depending upon the plan, you may be eligible to receive them sooner.

12.12 Am I entitled to cost-of-living increases on my share of my spouse's retirement?

It depends. If your spouse has a retirement plan that includes a provision for a *cost-of-living allowance (COLA),* talk to your attorney about whether or not this can be included in the court order dividing the retirement.

12.13 What circumstances might prevent me from receiving part of my spouse's retirement benefits?

Some government pension plans, if they are in lieu of a Social Security benefit, are not subject to division. If you or your spouse is employed by a government agency, talk with your attorney about whether or not you are entitled to any other retirement benefits and how this may affect the property settlement in your case.

12.14 Does the death of my spouse affect the payout of retirement benefits to me or to our children?

It depends upon both the nature of your spouse's retirement plan and the terms of the court order dividing the retirement. If you want to be eligible for survivorship benefits from your spouse's pension, discuss the issue with your attorney before your case is settled or goes to trial. He/she can advise you.

Some plans allow only a surviving spouse or former spouse to be a beneficiary. Others may allow for the naming of an alternate beneficiary, such as your children.

12.15 Can I still collect on my former spouse's Social Security benefits if he or she passes on before I do?

It depends. You may be eligible to receive benefits if:

- You were married to your spouse for ten or more years
- You are not remarried
- You are at least sixty-two-years old
- The benefit you would receive based on your own earning record is less than the benefit you would receive from your former spouse

For more information, contact your local Social Security Administration (SSA) office or visit the SSA website at: www.ssa.gov.

12.16 What orders might the court enter regarding life insurance?

The judge may order you or your spouse to maintain a life insurance policy to ensure that future support payments, such as child support and alimony (spousal support) are made. In most cases you will be required to pay for your own life insurance after your divorce, and you should include this as an expense in your monthly budget.

12.17 Because we share children, should I consider my spouse as a beneficiary on my life insurance?

It depends upon your intentions. If your intention is to give the money to your former spouse, by all means name the other parent as beneficiary.

However, if you intend the life insurance proceeds to be used for the benefit of your children, talk with your attorney about your options. You may consider naming a trustee to manage the life insurance proceeds on behalf of your children, and there may be reasons to choose someone other than your former spouse.

12.18 Can the court require in the final decree of dissolution of marriage that I be the beneficiary of my spouse's insurance policy, so long as the children are minors or indefinitely?

When a court order is entered for life insurance, it is ordinarily for the purposes of ensuring payment of future support and will terminate when the support obligation has ended. Naming you as the beneficiary on your spouse's insurance policy for purposes of ensuring payment of future child support is one option. The court may also name the children directly as beneficiaries, or require a trust be established to receive the life insurance proceeds on behalf of your children.

12.19 My spouse is in the military. What are my rights to benefits after the divorce?

As the former spouse of a military member, the types of benefits to which you may be entitled are typically determined by the number of years you were married, the number of years your spouse was in the military while you were married, and whether or not you have remarried. Be sure you obtain accurate information about these dates.

Among the benefits for which you may be eligible are:

- A portion of your spouse's military retirement pay
- A survivor benefit in the event of your spouse's death
- Health care or participation in a temporary, transitional health care program
- Ability to keep your military identification card
- Use of certain military facilities, such as the commissary

Although your divorce is pending, educate yourself about your right to future military benefits so that you can plan for your future with clarity. If your divorce is still pending, contact your base legal office, or, for more information, visit the website for the branch of the military of which your spouse was a member.

13

Division of Debts

Throughout a marriage, most couples will have disagreements about money from time to time. You might think extra money should be spent on a family vacation, but your spouse might insist it should be saved for your retirement. You might think it's time to finally buy a new car, but your spouse thinks you driving the ten-year-old van for two more years is a better idea.

If you and your spouse had different philosophies about saving and spending during your marriage, chances are you will have some differing opinions when dividing your debts in divorce. What you both can count on is that New Mexico law provides that, to reach a fair outcome, the payment of debts must also be taken into consideration when dividing the assets from your marriage.

There are steps you can take to ensure the best outcome possible when it comes to dividing your marital debt. These include providing accurate and complete debt information to your attorney and asking your attorney to include provisions in your final decree of dissolution of marriage to protect you in the future if your spouse refuses to pay his/her share.

Regardless of how the debts from your marriage are divided, know that you will gradually build your independent financial success when making a fresh start after your divorce is final.

13.1 Who is responsible for paying credit card bills and making house payments during the divorce proceedings?

In most cases, the court will not make decisions regarding the payment of credit card debt on a temporary basis. Work with your attorney and your spouse to reach a temporary agreement. Discuss the importance of making at least minimum payments on time to avoid substantial finance charges and late fees.

Typically the spouse who remains in the home will be responsible for the mortgage payments, taxes, utilities, and most other ordinary house expenses.

If you are concerned that you cannot afford to stay in the marital home on a temporary basis, talk with your attorney about your options prior to your temporary hearing.

13.2 What, if anything, should I be doing with the credit card companies as we go through the divorce?

If possible, it is best to obtain some separate credit prior to the divorce. This will help you establish credit in your own name and help you with necessary purchases following a separation.

Begin by obtaining a copy of your credit report from at least two of the three nationwide consumer reporting companies: Experian, Equifax, or TransUnion. The Fair Credit Reporting Act entitles you to a free copy of your credit report from each of these three companies every twelve months. To order your free annual report online, go to www.AnnualCreditReport.com, call toll-free to (877) 322-8228, or complete an Annual Credit Report Request Form and mail it to: Annual Credit Report Request Service, P.O. Box 105281, Atlanta, Georgia 30348-5281. You can print the form from the Federal Trade Commission website at www.ftc.gov/credit.

Your spouse may have incurred debt using your name. This information is important to relay to your attorney. If you and your spouse have joint credit card accounts, contact each credit card company to close the account. Do the same if your spouse is an authorized user on any of your accounts. Be sure to let your spouse know if you close an account he or she has been using.

If you want to maintain credit with a company, ask to have a new account in your own name.

13.3   How is credit card debt divided?

Credit card debt will be divided as a part of the overall division of the marital property and debts. Just as in the division of property, the court considers what is equitable, or fair, in your case.

If your spouse has exclusively used a credit card for purposes that did not benefit the family, such as gambling, talk with your attorney. In most cases the court will not review a lengthy history of how you and your spouse used the credit cards, but there can be exceptions.

13.4   Am I responsible for repayment of my spouse's student loans?

It depends. If your spouse incurred student loans prior to the marriage, it is most likely that he or she will be ordered to pay that debt.

If the debt was incurred during the marriage, how the funds were used may have an impact on who is ordered to pay them. For example, if your spouse borrowed $3,000 during the marriage for tuition, it is likely your spouse will be ordered to pay that debt. However, if a $3,000 student loan was taken out by your spouse, but $1,000 of it was used for a family vacation, then the court would be more likely to order the debt shared.

If you were a joint borrower on your spouse's student loan and your spouse fails to pay the loan, the lender may attempt to collect from you even if your spouse has been ordered to pay the debt.

If either you or your spouse has student loan debt, be sure to give your attorney the complete history regarding the debt and ask about the most likely outcome under the facts of your case.

13.5   During the divorce proceedings, am I still responsible for debt my spouse continues to accrue?

It depends. In most cases the court will order each of the parties to be responsible for his/her own post-separation debts. In some cases, the date for dividing debt is when the parties separated households; in others, it is the date the petition for dissolution of marriage was filed.

13.6 During the marriage my spouse applied for and received several credit cards without my knowledge. Am I responsible for them?

It depends. The court will consider the overall fairness of the property and debt division when deciding who should pay this debt. If your spouse bought items with the cards and intends to keep those items, it is likely that he or she will be ordered to pay the debt incurred for the purchases.

The credit card companies are unlikely to be able to pursue collection from you for the debt unless your spouse used them for the necessities of life, such as food, necessary clothing, or housing.

13.7 During our marriage, we paid off thousands of dollars of debt incurred by my spouse before we were married. Will the court take this into consideration when dividing our property and debt?

It might. Just as premarital assets can have an impact on the overall division of property and debts, so can premarital debt. Depending upon the length of the marriage, the evidence of the debt, and the amount paid, it may be a factor for the judge to consider.

Be sure to let your attorney know if either you or your spouse brought substantial debt into the marriage.

13.8 Regarding debts, what is a *hold-harmless clause,* and why should it be in the divorce decree?

A *hold-harmless provision* is intended to protect you in the event that your spouse fails to follow a court order to pay a debt after the divorce is granted. The language typically provides that your spouse shall "indemnify and hold [you] harmless from liability" on the debt.

If you and your spouse have a joint debt and your spouse fails to pay, the creditor may nevertheless attempt to collect from you. This is because the court is without power to change the creditor's rights and can make orders affecting only you and your spouse.

182

Division of Debts

In the event your spouse fails to pay a court-ordered debt and the creditor attempts collection from you, the hold-harmless provision in your final decree of dissolution of marriage can be used in an effort to insist that payment is made by your former spouse.

13.9 Why do my former spouse's doctors say they have a legal right to collect from me when my former spouse was ordered to pay her own medical bills?

Under New Mexico law, you may be held liable for the "necessities of life" of your spouse, such as health care. Your final decree of dissolution of marriage does not take away the legal rights of creditors to collect debts. Contact your attorney about your rights to enforce the court order that your spouse pays his/her own medical bills.

13.10 My spouse and I have agreed that I will keep our home; why must I refinance the mortgage?

There may be a number of reasons why your spouse is asking you to refinance the mortgage. First, the mortgage company cannot be forced to take your spouse's name off of the mortgage note. This means that if you did not make the house payments, the lender could pursue collection against your spouse.

Second, your spouse may want to receive their share of the home equity. It may be possible for you to borrow additional money at the time of refinancing to pay your spouse his/her share of the equity in the home.

Third, the mortgage on your family home may prevent your spouse from buying a home in the future. Because there remains a risk that your spouse could be pursued for the debt to the mortgage company, it is unlikely that a second lender will want to take the risk of extending further credit to your spouse.

13.11 Can I file for bankruptcy while my divorce is pending?

Yes. Consult with your attorney if you are considering filing for bankruptcy while your divorce is pending. It will be important for you to ask yourself a number of questions, such as:

183

- Should I file for bankruptcy on my own or with my spouse?
- How will filing for bankruptcy affect my ability to purchase a home in the future?
- Which debts can be discharged in bankruptcy, and which cannot?
- How will a bankruptcy affect the division of property and debts in the divorce?
- How might a delay in the divorce proceeding due to a bankruptcy impact my case?
- What form of bankruptcy is best for my situation?

If you use a different attorney for your bankruptcy than you have for your divorce, be sure that each attorney is kept fully informed about the developments in the other case.

13.12 What happens if my spouse files for bankruptcy during our divorce?

Contact your attorney right away. Filing for bankruptcy while your divorce is pending can have a significant impact on your divorce. Your attorney can advise you whether or not certain debts are likely to be discharged in the bankruptcy, the delay a bankruptcy may cause to your divorce, and whether or not bankruptcy is an appropriate option for you.

13.13 Can I file for divorce while I am in bankruptcy?

Yes. However, you must receive the bankruptcy court's permission to proceed with the divorce. Although in bankruptcy, your property is protected from debt collection by the "automatic stay." The stay can also prevent the divorce court from dividing property between you and your spouse until you obtain the bankruptcy court's permission to proceed with the divorce.

13.14 What should I do if my former spouse files for bankruptcy after our divorce?

Contact your attorney immediately. If you learn that your former spouse has filed for bankruptcy, you may have certain rights to object to the discharge of any debts your spouse was ordered to pay under your divorce decree. If you fail to take action, it is possible that you will be held responsible for debts your spouse was ordered to pay.

13.15 If I am awarded child support or alimony in my decree, can these obligations be discharged if my former spouse files for bankruptcy after our divorce?

No. Support obligations such as child support and alimony are not dischargeable in bankruptcy, meaning these debts cannot be eliminated in a bankruptcy proceeding.

13.16 What happens if my former spouse does not pay their obligations as assigned in the final decree of dissolution of marriage?

If your former spouse does not pay the debts assigned to him or her in the final decree of dissolution of marriage, you may be able to pursue a contempt of court action. A party is in contempt of court if they willfully disobey or disregard a court order. Talk with your attorney to determine whether a contempt of court action may be filed in your case to enforce your rights under your final decree of dissolution of marriage.

14

Taxes

A number of tax issues may arise in your divorce. Your attorney may not be able to answer all of your tax questions, so consulting your accountant or tax advisor for additional advice might be necessary.

Taxes are an important consideration in both settlement negotiations and trial preparation. They should not be overlooked. Taxes can impact many of your decisions, including those regarding alimony, division of property, and the receipt of benefits. It is important to know the tax implications of the property division and spousal support agreements you are considering before you enter into any final agreement. Many courts are not equipped, nor is it their responsibility, to understand all of the tax implications of a property division or a spousal support award.

Perhaps more so than in any other area of law, tax law changes constantly. Everything included herein should be checked with your attorney and tax advisor to be sure it is still correct and current at the time of your divorce.

14.1 Will either my spouse or I have to pay income tax when we transfer property or pay a property settlement to each other according to our final decree of dissolution of marriage?

No. However, it is important that you see the future tax consequences of a subsequent withdrawal, sale, or transfer of certain assets you receive in your divorce. Consider such things as capital gains tax on the sale of property in the future. This is very important especially if the sale of an asset is imminent. At the very least, be aware of the difference in *pretax* assets and *posttax* assets, and be wary about trading one for the other.

The point is that what you get in a property division may not always be what you get to keep. It is important to ask your attorney to take tax consequences into consideration when looking at the division of your assets. You should be sure that you understand the actual meaning of the terms being used, and the values of the assets being distributed.

14.2   Is the child support I pay tax deductible?

No. Child support is not tax deductible by the paying parent nor is it income to the parent receiving the support.

14.3   Is the amount of spousal support I am ordered to pay tax deductible?

Probably. Spousal support paid pursuant to a court order is normally deductible, unless the court specifies or the parties agree that it is not to be tax deductible. Spousal support is generally tax deductible if:

- You and your spouse or former spouse do not file a joint return with each other
- The payment is in cash (including checks or money orders)
- The payment is received by (or on behalf of) your spouse or former spouse
- You and your former spouse are not members of the same household when you make the payment
- You have no liability to make the payment (in cash or property) after the death of your spouse or former spouse
- Your payment is not treated as child support or a property settlement
- Your payment is not interim support paid during the pendency of the divorce

14.4 Do I have to pay tax on the spousal support I receive?

Probably. You must pay income tax on the spousal support you receive, unless the court specifies or the parties agree that it is not to be included in the recipient's income. This will include court-ordered spousal support and may also include other forms of spousal support, such as payments to a third party for the benefit of the spouse if ordered to do so, but not child support, paid by your spouse.

Income tax is a critical factor in determining a fair amount of alimony. If there is a difference in postdivorce tax rates between the parties, it is possible in many cases to increase the amount of spousal support received by the alimony recipient while not increasing the amount spent by the payor. Insist that your attorney bring this issue to the attention of your spouse's attorney, or to the judge, if your case proceeds to trial, so that both the tax you pay and the deduction your spouse receives are taken into consideration.

Be sure to consult with your tax advisor about payment of tax on your spousal support. Making estimated tax payments throughout the year or withholding additional taxes from your wages can avoid a burdensome tax liability at the end of the year. It is important to budget for these taxes.

Taxes are also another item to consider when looking at your monthly living expenses for the purposes of seeking an alimony award.

14.5 Is there anything else I should know about spousal support and taxes?

If your spousal support payments to your spouse decrease or end during the first three calendar years after your divorce, you may be subject to the recapture rule. You are subject to the *recapture rule* if the spousal support you pay in the third year decreases by more than $15,000 from the second year, or if the spousal support you pay in the second and third year decreases significantly from the spousal support you pay in the first year. If you are subject to this rule, you must claim a portion of the spousal support payments you've previously deducted as income in the third year. Likewise, the recipient can deduct part of the spousal support payments he or she previously claimed as income in the third year. The recapture calculation can be very complicated and you should consult a tax professional to ensure that you are not affected by this rule.

14.6 During the divorce proceedings, is our tax filing status affected?

It can be. The date you file for divorce is not relevant to your tax filing status. However, the date of the divorce is relevant. If your final decree of dissolution of marriage is entered by December 31 of the tax year, then you are considered unmarried for that tax year.

If you are considered unmarried, your filing status is either "single" or, under certain circumstances, "head of household." If your decree is not final as of December 31, your filing status is either "married filing a joint return" or "married filing a separate return," unless you live apart from your spouse and meet the exception for "head of household."

While your divorce is in progress, talk to both your tax advisor and your attorney about your filing status. It may be beneficial to figure your tax on both a joint return and a separate return to see which gives you the lower tax. IRS Publication 504, Divorced or Separated Individuals, provides more detail on tax issues while you are going through a divorce.

14.7 Should I file a joint income tax return with my spouse while our divorce is pending?

Consult your tax advisor to determine the risks and benefits of filing a joint return with your spouse. Compare this with the consequences of filing your tax return separately. Often the overall tax liability will be less with the filing of a joint return, but there are other considerations, including any concerns you have about the accuracy and truthfulness of the information on the tax return. Further, because New Mexico is a community property state, the income received by both parties while the divorce is pending is considered community income and according to IRS regulations that income should be divided between the parties if filing separate returns.

If you have any doubts, consult both your attorney and your tax advisor before agreeing to sign a joint tax return with your spouse. Prior to filing a return with your spouse, try to reach agreement about how any tax owed or refund expected will be shared, and ask your attorney to assist you in getting this in writing to avoid future disputes.

14.8 My spouse will not cooperate in providing the necessary documents to prepare or file our taxes jointly. What options do I have?

Talk with your attorney about requesting your spouse to cooperate in the preparation and filing your joint return. Although a judge cannot order your spouse to sign a joint return, he/she may be able to penalize them for their unreasonable refusal to do so or for their failure to provide you with the documents necessary to enable you to file a separate return.

14.9 For tax purposes, is one time of year better to divorce than another?

It depends upon your tax situation. If you and your spouse agree that it would be beneficial to file joint tax returns for the year in which you are divorcing, you may wish to not have your divorce finalized before the end of the year, but rather delay entry of the final decree of dissolution of marriage to the first part of the next year.

Your marital status for filing income taxes is determined by your status on December 31.

14.10 What tax consequences should I consider regarding the sale of our home?

When your home is sold, whether during your divorce or after, the sale may be subject to a capital gains tax. Under recent rules, if your home was your primary residence and you lived in the home for two of the preceding five years, you may be eligible to exclude up to $250,000 of the gain on the sale of your home. If both you and your spouse meet the ownership and residence tests, you may be eligible to exclude up to $500,000 of the gain. Again, these rules may be subject to change at any time.

If you anticipate the gain on the sale of your residence to be more than $250,000, talk with your attorney early in the divorce process about a plan to minimize the tax liability. For more information, see IRS Publication 523, Selling Your Home, or visit the IRS website at www.irs.gov and talk with your tax advisor.

14.11 How might capital gains tax be a problem for me years after the divorce?

Future capital gains tax on the sale of property should be discussed with your attorney during the negotiation and trial preparation stages of your case. This is especially important if the sale of the property is imminent. Failure to do so may result in an unfair outcome.

For example, suppose you agree that your spouse will be awarded the proceeds from the sale of your home valued at $200,000, after the real estate commission, and you will take the stock portfolio also valued at $200,000.

Suppose that after the divorce, you decide to sell the stock. It is still valued at $200,000, but you learn that its original price was $120,000 and that you must pay capital gains tax of 15 percent on the $80,000 of gain. You pay tax of $12,000, leaving you with $188,000.

Meanwhile, your former spouse sells the marital home but pays no capital gains tax because he qualifies for the $250,000 exemption. He is left with the full $200,000.

There are many variations to this type of scenario, but they all demonstrate that taxes matter in the value of the assets distributed upon your divorce. Tax implications of your property division should always be discussed with your attorney, with support from your tax advisor as needed.

14.12 During and after the divorce, who gets to claim the children as dependents?

This issue should be addressed in settlement negotiations or at trial, if settlement is not reached. Each dependency exemption can be worth a significant amount and the allocation of the exemptions needs to be addressed as part of your negotiations. Under the Internal Revenue Code, the primary custodial parent may claim the children as an exemption.

In New Mexico, under current law, a judge has discretion to determine who will be entitled to claim the child or children as exemptions for income tax purposes. Where child support has been ordered pursuant to the New Mexico Child Support Guidelines, judges may order that the exemptions be shared or alternated. As part of that award, however, most judges will order that the payor of child support be current on his/her child-support obligation to be eligible to claim the income tax dependency exemption. Additionally, if one party has income so low or so high that he or she will not benefit from the dependency exemption, the court may award the exemption to the other parent. It might make sense to trade the dependency exemptions to the other parent for additional support or property.

14.13 My final decree of dissolution of marriage says I have to sign IRS Form 8332 so my former spouse can claim our child as an exemption, because I have custody. Should I sign it once for all future years?

Probably not. Child custody and child support can be modified in the future. If there is a future modification of custody or support, which parent is entitled to claim the child as an exemption could change. The best practice is to provide your former spouse a timely copy of Form 8332 (Release/Revocation of Release of Claim to Exemption for Child by Custodial Parent) signed by you for the appropriate tax year only, one year at a time, if still appropriate.

14.14 Can my spouse and I split the child-care tax credit?

Only the custodial parent is allowed to claim the credit. If you are a noncustodial parent and paying child care, talk to your attorney about how to address this issue in your final decree of dissolution of marriage.

14.15 Is the cost of getting a divorce, including my attorney fees, tax deductible under any circumstances?

Your legal fees for getting a divorce are not deductible. However, a portion of your attorney fees may be deductible if they are for:

- The collection of sums included in your gross income, such as alimony or interest income
- Advice regarding the determination of taxes or tax due

Attorney fees are "miscellaneous" deductions for individuals and are consequently limited to 2 percent of your adjusted gross income. More details can be found in IRS Publication 529, Miscellaneous Deductions.

You may also be able to deduct fees you pay to appraisers or accountants who help. Talk to your tax advisor about whether or not any portion of your attorney fees or other expenses from your divorce are deductible.

14.16 Do I have to complete a new Form W-4 for my employer because of my divorce?

Completing a new Form W-4, Employee's Withholding Allowance Certificate, will help you to claim the proper withholding allowances based upon your marital status and exemptions. Also, if you are receiving spousal support, you may need to make quarterly estimated tax payments. Consult with your tax advisor to ensure you are making the most preferable tax planning decision.

14.17 What is *innocent spouse relief* and how can it help me?

Innocent spouse relief refers to a method of obtaining relief from the Internal Revenue Service for taxes owed as a result of a joint income tax return filed during your marriage. If you filed a joint return, and your spouse made misrepresentations regarding his/her income, the innocent spouse protection may relieve you from responsibility for the liability. Numerous factors affect your eligibility for innocent spouse tax relief, such as:

- You would suffer a financial hardship if you were required to pay the tax.
- You did not significantly benefit from the unpaid taxes.
- You suffered abuse during your marriage.
- You thought your spouse would pay the taxes on the original return.

Talk with your attorney or your tax advisor if you are concerned about liability for taxes arising from joint tax returns filed during the marriage. You may benefit from a referral to an attorney who specializes in tax law.

15

Going to Court

For many of us, our images of going to court are created by movie scenes and our favorite television shows. We picture the witness breaking down in tears after a grueling cross-examination. We see attorneys strutting around the court-room, waving their arms as they plead their case to the jury.

Hollywood drama, however, is a far cry from reality. Going to court for your divorce can mean many things, ranging from sitting in a hallway while waiting for the attorneys and judges to conclude a conference, to being on the witness stand giving mundane answers to questions about your monthly living expenses.

Regardless of the nature of your court proceeding, going to court often evokes a sense of anxiety. Perhaps your divorce might be the first time in your life that you have even been in a courtroom. Be assured that these feelings of nervousness and uncertainty are normal.

Understanding what will occur in court and being well prepared for any court hearings will relieve much of your stress. Knowing the order of events, the role of the people in the courtroom, etiquette in the courtroom, and what is expect-ed of you will make the entire experience easier.

Your attorney will be with you to support you any time you go to court. Remember, every court appearance moves you one step closer to completing your divorce so that you can move forward with your life.

15.1 What do I need to know about appearing in court and court dates in general?

Court dates are important. As soon as you receive a notice from your attorney about a court date in your case, confirm whether your attendance will be required and mark the date on your calendar.

Ask your attorney about the nature of the hearing, including whether or not the judge will be listening to testimony by witnesses or merely listening to the arguments of the attorneys.

Ask whether it is necessary for you to meet with your attorney or take any other action to prepare for the hearing, such as providing additional information or documents.

Find out how long the hearing is expected to last. It may be as short as a few minutes or as long as a day or more.

If you plan to attend the hearing, determine where and when to meet your attorney. Depending upon the type of hearing, your attorney may want you to arrive in advance of the scheduled hearing time to prepare.

Make sure you know the location of the courthouse, where to park, whether you may have a cell phone, and the floor and room number of the courtroom. Planning for such simple matters as having change for a parking meter can eliminate unnecessary stress. If you want someone to go to court with you to provide support, check with your attorney first.

15.2 When and how often will I need to go to court?

When and how often you will need to go to court will be determined by a number of factors. Depending upon the complexity of your case, you may have only one court hearing or numerous hearings throughout the course of your divorce.

Some hearings, usually those on procedural matters, are attended only by the attorneys. These could include requests for the other side to provide information or for the setting of certain deadlines. These hearings are often brief and do not require witness testimony. Other hearings, such as temporary hearings for custody or support, are typically attended by both parties and their attorneys.

If you and your spouse settle all of the issues in your case, you will likely never have to step foot in the courthouse.

If your case proceeds to trial, your appearance will be required for the duration of the trial. In New Mexico, divorce matters are heard before a judge only; juries do not hear divorces.

15.3   How much notice will I receive about appearing in court?

The amount of notice you will receive for any court hearing can vary from a few days to several weeks. Ask your attorney whether and when it will be necessary for you to appear in court on your case so that you can have ease in preparing and planning.

If you receive a notice of a hearing, contact your attorney immediately. He/she can tell you whether your appearance is required and what other steps are needed to prepare.

15.4   I am afraid to be alone in the same room with my spouse. When I go to court, is this going to happen?

Talk to your attorney. Prior to any court hearing, you and your spouse may be asked to wait while your attorneys meet with the judge and/or one another to discuss preliminary matters or possible settlement options.

A number of things can be done to ensure that you feel safe. These might include having you and your spouse wait in different locations or having a friend or family member present.

Your attorney wants to support you in feeling secure throughout all court proceedings. Just let him or her know your concerns.

15.5   My spouse's attorney keeps asking for continuances of court dates. Is there anything I can do to stop this?

Continuances, or postponements, of court dates are not unusual in divorces. A court date might be postponed for many reasons, including a conflict on the calendar of one of the attorneys or the judge, the lack of availability of one of the parties or an important witness, or the need for information or more time to prepare.

Discuss with your attorney your desire to move your case forward without further delay, so that repeated requests for continuances can be minimized.

15.6   If I have to go to court, will I be put on the stand? Will there be a jury?

In New Mexico, divorce matters are heard before a judge only; juries do not hear divorces. Whether or not you will be put on the stand will depend upon the nature of the issues in dispute, the judge assigned to your case, and your attorney's strategy for your case.

15.7   My attorney said I need to be in court for our temporary hearing next week. What's going to happen?

A temporary hearing is held to determine such matters as who remains in the house while your divorce is pending, temporary physical custody of the children, temporary support, and other financial matters.

The procedure for your temporary hearing can vary depending upon the county in which your case was filed, the judge to which the case is assigned, and whether or not temporary custody is disputed.

Even if testimony is not taken at your temporary hearing, your presence is still important. Your attorney may need additional information from you during the hearing, and last-minute negotiations to resolve temporary issues are not uncommon.

In some counties, your hearing will be one of numerous other hearings on the judge's calendar. You may find yourself in a courtroom with many other attorneys and their clients, all having matters scheduled before the court that day. Even though you are present in the courtroom, your attorney will make your argument to the judge and it is unlikely you will be required to provide formal testimony.

If temporary custody is disputed, you and other witnesses might be required to take the witness stand to give testimony at your temporary hearing. If this is the case, meeting with your attorney in advance to fully prepare is very important.

Talk to your attorney about the procedure you should expect for the temporary hearing in your case.

15.8 Do I have to go to court if all of the issues in my case are settled?

No. If you and your spouse settle all of the issues in your case, you can submit your final documents to the judge for his/her review and signature and never have to go to court.

15.9 Are there any rules about courtroom etiquette that I need to know?

Knowing a few tips about being in the courtroom will make your experience easier.

- Dress appropriately. Avoid overly casual dress, lots of jewelry, revealing clothing, and extreme hairstyles.
- Don't bring beverages into the courtroom. Most courts have rules that do not allow food and drink in courtrooms. If you need water, ask your attorney.
- Dispose of chewing gum before giving testimony.
- Don't talk aloud in the courtroom unless you're on the witness stand or being questioned by the judge.
- Stand up whenever the judge is entering or leaving the courtroom.
- Find out if electronic devices are allowed. If they are not, turn them off.
- Be mindful that the judge is likely observing you and those you bring to the hearing at all times.

Although you may feel anxious initially, you'll likely feel more relaxed about the courtroom setting once your hearing gets underway.

15.10 What is the role of the *bailiff*?

The *bailiff* provides support for the judge and attorneys in the management of the court calendar and the courtroom. He/she assists in the scheduling of court hearings and the management of legal documents given to the judge for review.

15.11 Will there be a *court reporter,* and what will he or she do?

A *court reporter* is a professional trained to make an accurate record of the words spoken and documents offered into evidence during court proceedings. Some counties use tape-recording devices in addition to or in lieu of court reporters.

A recorded transcript of a court proceeding may be purchased from the court. If your case is appealed, the transcript prepared by the court reporter will be used by the appeals court to review the facts of your case.

The court reporter is also responsible for managing documents and other items offered into evidence at trial.

Some hearings are held "off the record," which means that the court reporter is not making a record of what is being said. Ordinarily these are matters for which no appeal is expected to be taken.

15.12 Will I be able to talk to my attorney while we are in court?

During court proceedings it is important that your attorney give his/her attention to anything being said by the judge, witnesses, or your spouse's attorney. For this reason, your attorney may avoid talking with you when someone else in the courtroom is speaking.

Plan to have pen and paper with you when you go to court. If your court proceeding is underway and your attorney is listening to what is being said by others in the courtroom, write him/her a note with your questions or comments.

It is critical that your attorney hear each question asked by the other attorney and all answers given by each witness. If not, opportunities for making objections to inappropriate evidence may be lost. You can support your attorney in doing an effective job for you by minimizing the amount of talking you do to him or her while a court hearing is in progress.

If your court hearing is lengthy, breaks will be taken. You can use this time to discuss with your attorney any questions or observations you have about the proceeding.

15.13 What questions might my attorney ask me about the problems in our marriage and why I want the divorce?

Because New Mexico is a no-fault state, it is unlikely that you will be asked any questions about the nature of the marital problems that led to the divorce.

15.14 My attorney said that the judge has issued a *pretrial order* having to do with my upcoming trial and that we'll have to comply with it. What does this mean?

Ask your attorney for a copy of the *pretrial order.* Some judges will order that certain information be provided either to the opposing party or to the judge in advance of trial. This might include:

- A list of issues that have been settled
- A list of issues that are still disputed
- Agreements, referred to as stipulations, as to the truth of certain facts
- The names of witnesses
- Exhibits
- A summary of how you want the judge to decide the case
- Deadlines for providing the information

15.15 What is a *pretrial conference*?

A *pretrial conference* is a meeting held with the attorneys and the judge to review information related to an upcoming trial, such as:

- How long the trial is expected to last
- The issues in dispute
- The law surrounding the disputed issues
- The identification of witnesses
- Trial exhibits
- The status of negotiations

Often the trial date is set at the pretrial conference. If a pretrial conference is held in your case, ask your attorney whether you should attend. Your attorney may request that you either be present for the conference or be available by phone.

15.16 Besides meeting with my attorney, is there anything else I should do to prepare for my upcoming trial?

Yes. Be sure to review your deposition and any information you provided in your discovery, such as answers to interrogatories. Also be sure to review any affidavits previously submitted to the judge, such as your interim monthly income and expenses statement prepared for your interim hearing. At trial, it is possible that you will be asked some of the same questions. If you think you might give different answers at trial, discuss this with your attorney. It is important that your attorney know in advance of trial whether any information you provided during the discovery process has changed.

15.17 I'm meeting with my attorney to prepare for trial. How do I make the most of these meetings?

Meeting with your attorney to prepare for your trial is important to achieving a good outcome. Come to the meeting prepared to discuss the following:

- The issues in your case
- Your desired outcome on each of the issues
- The questions you might be asked at trial by both attorneys
- The exhibits that will be offered into evidence during the trial
- The witnesses for your trial
- The status of negotiations

Your meeting with your attorney will help you better understand what to expect at your trial and make the trial experience easier.

15.18 My attorney says that the law firm is busy with trial preparation. What exactly is my attorney doing to prepare for my trial?

Countless tasks are necessary to perform to prepare your case for trial. These are just some of them:

- Developing arguments to be made on each of the contested issues
- Researching and reviewing the relevant law in your case

- Reviewing the facts of your case to determine which witnesses are best suited to testifying about them
- Reviewing, selecting, and preparing exhibits
- Preparing questions for all witnesses
- Preparing an opening statement and closing argument
- Reviewing rules on evidence to prepare for any objections to be made or opposed at trial
- Determining the order of witnesses and all exhibits
- Preparing your file for the day in court, including preparing a trial notebook with essential information

Your attorney is committed to a good outcome for you in your divorce. He/she will be engaged in many important actions to fully prepare your case for trial.

15.19   How do I know who my witnesses will be at trial?

Well in advance of your trial date, your attorney will discuss with you whether other witnesses, besides you and your spouse, will be necessary. Witnesses can include family members, friends, child-care providers, and so on. When thinking of potential witnesses, consider your relationship with the witness, whether or not that witness has had an opportunity to observe relevant facts, and whether or not the witness has knowledge different from that of other witnesses.

You may also have expert witnesses testify on your behalf. An expert witness will provide opinion testimony based upon specialized knowledge, training, or experience. For example, a psychologist, real estate appraiser, or accountant may provide expert testimony on your behalf.

15.20   My divorce is scheduled for trial. Does this mean there is no hope for a settlement?

Many cases are settled after a trial date is set. The setting of a trial date may cause you and your spouse to think about the risks and costs of going to trial. This can help you and your spouse focus on what is most important to you and lead you toward a negotiated settlement. Because the costs of preparing for and proceeding to trial are substantial, it is best to engage in settlement negotiations well in advance of your trial date.

However, it is not uncommon for cases to settle a few days before trial, or even at the courthouse before your trial begins.

15.21 Can I prevent my spouse from being in the courtroom?

Probably not. Because your spouse has a legal interest in the outcome of your divorce, he/she has a right to be present. New Mexico courtrooms are open to the public. Consequently, it is not uncommon for persons not involved in your divorce to pass through the courtroom at various times simply because they have other business with the court.

15.22 Can I take a friend or family member with me to court?

Let your attorney know in advance if you intend to bring anyone to court with you. Some people important to you may be very emotional about your divorce or your spouse. Be sure to invite someone who is better able to focus attention on supporting you rather than on his/her own feelings.

It is also important to know whether the person you intend to bring will be called as a witness. In most cases where witnesses other than the spouses are testifying, the attorneys request that the court sequester, or isolate, the witnesses. The judge then orders all witnesses, except you and your spouse, to leave the courtroom until after they have testified. Once a witness has completed his/her testimony, he/she will ordinarily be allowed to remain in the courtroom for the remainder of the trial.

15.23 I want to do a great job testifying as a witness in my divorce trial. What are some tips?

Keep the following in mind to be a good witness on your own behalf:

- Tell the truth. Although this may not be always be comfortable, it is critical if you want your testimony to be believed by the judge.
- Listen carefully to the complete question before thinking of your answer. Wait to consider your answer until the full question is asked.
- Slow down. It's easy to speed up our speech when we are anxious. Taking your time with your answers

ensures that the judge hears you and that the court reporter can accurately record your testimony.

- If you don't understand a question or don't know the answer, be sure to say so.
- If the question calls for a "yes" or "no" answer, simply say so. Then wait for the attorney to ask you the next question. If there is more you want to explain, remember that you have already told your attorney all the important facts and he or she will make sure you are allowed to give any testimony significant in your case.
- Don't argue with the judge or the attorneys.
- Take your time. You may be asked some questions that call for a thoughtful response. If you need a moment to reflect on an answer before you give it, allow yourself that time.
- Stop speaking if an objection is made by one of the attorneys. Wait until the judge has decided whether to allow you to answer.
- If you begin to feel emotional, your attorney can ask for a short break

15.24 Should I be worried about being cross-examined by my spouse's attorney at trial?

If your case goes to trial, prepare to be asked some questions by your spouse's attorney. Many of these questions will call for a simple "yes" or "no."

If you are worried about particular questions, discuss your concerns with your attorney. He/she can support you in giving a truthful response. Focus on preparing well for being asked questions by your spouse's attorney. Try not to take the questions personally; remember that the attorney is fulfilling a duty to advocate for your spouse's interests. Remember that you are just doing your best to tell the truth about the facts.

15.25 What happens on the day of trial?

Although no two trials are alike, the following steps will occur in most divorce trials:

- Attorneys give opening statements.

- Petitioner's attorney calls petitioner's witnesses to testify.
- Respondent's attorney may cross-examine each of them.
- Respondent's attorney calls respondent's witnesses to testify.
- Petitioner's attorney may cross-examine each of them.
- Petitioner's attorney calls any rebuttal witnesses, that is, witnesses whose testimony contradicts the testimony of the respondent's witnesses.
- Closing arguments made first by the petitioner's attorney and then by the respondent's attorney.

15.26 Will the judge decide my case the day I go to court?

Possibly. Often there is so much information from the trial for the judge to consider that it is not possible for the judge to give an immediate ruling.

The judge may want to review documents, review the law, perform calculations, review his/her notes, and give thoughtful consideration to the issues to be decided. For this reason, it may be days, weeks, or in some cases, even longer before a ruling is made.

When a judge does not make a ruling immediately upon the conclusion of a trial, it is said that the case has been "taken under advisement."

16

The Appeals Process

You may find that despite your best efforts to settle your case, your divorce went to trial and the judge made major decisions that will have a serious impact on your future. You may be either gravely disappointed or even shocked by the judge's ruling.

The judge might have seen your case differently than you and your attorney did. Perhaps the judge made mistakes. Or it may be that New Mexico law simply does not allow for the outcome you were hoping for.

Whatever the reasons for the court's rulings, you may feel that the judge's decisions are not ones that you can live with. If this is the case, talk to your attorney immediately about your right to appeal. Together you can decide whether an appeal is in your best interest, or whether it is better to accept the court's ruling and invest your energy in moving forward with your future without an appeal.

16.1 How much time after my divorce do I have to file an appeal?

You must file an appeal within thirty days of the final order you wish to appeal. Because your attorney may also recommend filing certain motions following your trial, discuss your appeal rights with your attorney as soon as you have received the judge's ruling.

A timely discussion with your attorney about your right to appeal is essential so important deadlines are not missed.

16.2   Can I appeal a temporary order?

No. Under New Mexico law, only final orders may be appealed.

16.3   What parts of the final decree of dissolution of marriage can be appealed?

If you or your spouse is unhappy with final decisions made by the judge in your case, either of you can file an appeal. Decisions that can be appealed include custody, parenting time, child support, alimony, whether property is separate or community, division of property, value of property, and attorney's fees.

16.4   Will my attorney recommend I appeal specific aspects of the final decree of dissolution of marriage, or will I have to request it?

Your attorney may counsel you to file an appeal on certain issues of your case; you may also ask your attorney whether or not there is a legitimate basis for an appeal of any decision you believe is wrong. Talk to your attorney regarding the decisions most dissatisfying to you. Your attorney can advise you regarding which issues have the greatest likelihood of success on appeal, in light of the facts of your case and New Mexico law.

16.5   When should an appeal be filed?

An appeal should be filed only after careful consultation with your attorney when you believe that the judge has made a serious error under the law or the facts of your case. Among the factors you and your attorney should discuss are:

- Whether or not the judge had the authority under the law to make the decisions set forth in your final decree of dissolution of marriage
- The likelihood of the success of your appeal
- The risk that an appeal by you will encourage an appeal by your former spouse
- The cost of the appeal
- The length of time an appeal can be expected to take
- The impact of a delay in the case during the appeal

The deadline for filing an appeal is thirty days from the date that a final order is entered in your case. It is important that you are clear about the deadline that applies in your case, so talk to your attorney at once if you are thinking about an appeal.

16.6   Are there any disadvantages to filing an appeal?
There can be disadvantages to filing an appeal, including:

- Uncertainty as to the outcome
- Increase attorney's fees and costs
- The risks of a worse outcome on appeal than you received at trial
- Delay in finalizing your divorce
- Prolonged conflict between you and your former spouse
- Risk of a second trial occurring after the appeal
- Difficulty in obtaining closure and moving forward with your life

16.7   Is an attorney necessary to appeal?
The appeals process is very detailed and specific, with set deadlines and specific court rules. Given the complex nature of the appellate process, you should have an attorney if you intend to file an appeal.

16.8   How long does the appeals process usually take?
It depends. An appeal can take anywhere from several months to several years. An appeal may also result in the appellate court requiring further proceedings by the trial court. This will result in further delay.

16.9   What are the steps in the appeals process?
There are many steps that your attorney will take on your behalf in the appeals process, including:

- Identifying the issues to be appealed
- Filing a notice with the court of your intent to appeal
- Obtaining the necessary court documents and trial exhibits to send to the appellate court

- Obtaining the audio recordings of the trial (testimony by witnesses, statements by the judge and the attorneys made in the presence of the court reporter)
- Performing legal research to support your arguments on appeal
- Preparing and filing a document known as a brief, which sets for the facts of the case and relevant law, complete with citations to court transcript, court documents, and prior cases
- Perhaps making an oral argument before the judges of the appellate court

16.10 Is filing and pursuing an appeal expensive?

Yes. In addition to filing fees and attorney fees, there is likely to be a substantial cost for the preparation of the transcript of the trial testimony.

16.11 If I do not file an appeal, can I ever go back to court to change my final decree of dissolution of marriage?

Certain aspects of a final decree of dissolution of marriage are not modifiable, such as the division of property and debts or the award of attorney fees. Other parts of your final decree, such as support or matters regarding the children, may be modified if there has been a material and substantial change in circumstances.

A modification of custody or parenting time for minor children will also require you to show that the change would be in their best interest.

If your final decree of dissolution of marriage did not provide for alimony or if it ordered that the alimony be non-modifiable, it is unlikely that you will have any basis for a modification. If you believe that you have a basis for a modification of your final decree, consult with your attorney.

17

Prenuptial and
Postnuptial Agreements

New Mexico law permits a couple contemplating marriage to enter into a contract prior to the marriage known as a *prenuptial agreement* or a *premarital agreement*. It is also sometimes referred to as an *antenuptial agreement*. This agreement is usually sought by one or both partners to be able to protect property or assets from the potential claims of division of property if a divorce occurs down the road.

Historically, the most common situation for a prenuptial agreement was one in which one or both of the spouses had children and wanted to preserve all or some of the property they owned prior to the new marriage for their children from a prior marriage. Today, there can be other reasons, including a desire to record, prior to the marriage, an agreement as to what separate property existed and its value prior to the marriage. A *postnuptial agreement* can have the same purposes as a prenuptial agreement, except it is signed after the marriage. Assuming these documents are properly prepared and executed, these agreements are usually enforceable and difficult to break.

The most important elements to having an enforceable, unbreakable prenuptial agreement are the following:

- Each person (prospective spouse or existing spouse) must have legal advice or, better yet, legal representation. The reason is that the fact of having legal advice or legal representation reduces a potential future claim that the agreement was obtained by coercion or force.
- There must be full, adequate, and complete disclosure of all assets, debts, and income. The reason that this is

210

necessary is to show the agreement was not secured by deceit or by any misrepresentation or coercion.

- The final important principle is that the agreement is not being finalized and executed too close to the wedding date. The reason for this is because today, many weddings are major financial investments by either of the spouses or their families. If a prenuptial agreement is proposed by one of the partners to the other at the last minute, particularly if one of the partners makes the signing of the prenuptial agreement a requirement to be able to marry, it creates an emotional and financial coercive situation. The musicians, the caterers, the flowers, and the invitations have all been ordered well in advance of the wedding date. To make signing an agreement a condition right before the wedding takes place is really putting the other party under duress. Because of this, many attorneys will not draft a prenuptial agreement if it is too close to the wedding date.

In contrast, the postnuptial agreement is an agreement that the marital partners execute *after* the marriage. Depending on the circumstances, a postnuptial agreement may be ideal because it relieves the pressure to execute an agreement prior to the wedding. However, there is also the possibility that, once married, one of the spouses may simply refuse to sign any such agreement. It is just as important for postnuptial agreements to be drafted and executed with both spouses having legal advice or legal representation and for the agreement to be fair and entered into without any duress or coercion.

New Mexico law assumes if you are an adult and you have voluntarily agreed to the terms of a contract like a prenuptial agreement or a postnuptial agreement, and you had legal advice, you are presumed to have known what you were doing when you signed the contract. In those cases, the court is likely to enforce the terms of the agreement. Full disclosure, representation, and an absence of duress, or coercion of any kind, including time pressure, are the keys to having the agreement enforced.

17.1 What subjects can be covered by a premarital agreement?

The partners may negotiate terms to cover any of the following:

- The rights and obligations of each of the parties in any of the property of either or both of them whenever and wherever acquired or located
- The right to buy, sell, use, transfer, exchange, abandon, lease, consume, expend, assign, create a security interest in, mortgage, encumber, dispose of, or otherwise manage and control property
- The disposition of property upon separation, divorce, death, or the occurrence or nonoccurrence of any other event
- The terms or modification of spousal support
- The making of a will, trust, or other arrangement to carry out the provisions of the agreement
- The ownership rights in and disposition of the death benefit from a life insurance policy
- The choice of law governing the construction of the agreement
- Any other matter, including their personal rights and obligations, not in violation of commonly accepted moral principles or the law in New Mexico

The law of prenuptial agreements is still developing in New Mexico. For example, an agreement that attempts to eliminate spousal support, or to predetermine a certain amount of child support, may be unenforceable under the law. Also, an agreement that attempts to bar a spouse from seeking custody of a child would likely be found to be against the law and not enforceable.

17.2 I hear prenuptial agreements are easy to break. Is this true?

No. These agreements, if prepared correctly, are nearly impossible to break. Do not enter into a prenuptial agreement thinking it will be unenforceable if you divorce. Make sure you fully understand the terms of any agreement, as you will likely be bound by it.

17.3 My friend entered into a prenuptial agreement and waived her right to spousal support. She now has cancer and can't work. Will this provision be binding?

This agreement was probably entered into in a state other than New Mexico. Under New Mexico law, prenuptial agreements cannot adversely affect a child or spouse's right to support, affect a parent's right to child custody, or affect a person's choice of where to live or freedom to pursue career opportunities. These would be considered against public policy of New Mexico.

If your friend's agreement was presented to a court in New Mexico and your friend met the requirements of receiving spousal support, the court may require her spouse to pay support to assist her.

17.4 My fiancé gave me an agreement to review and told me that his attorney will answer any of my questions. Is this a good idea?

This is a terrible idea. Your fiancé's attorney is concerned with protecting his/her client's interests, and not yours. Even if you know and trust the attorney, you should obtain your own independent attorney so that you fully understand all of the terms and implications of the agreement. These agreements significantly impact your financial future, and you shouldn't enter into the agreement without your own representation.

17.5 What exactly is the role of the attorney in a prenuptial agreement?

The attorney's role varies, depending upon the circumstances. If one of the parties initiates the agreement, that party's attorney will usually draft the agreement according to what their client has requested or based on discussions between the client and the attorney. After the initiating party has approved the agreement, it is sent to the other party's attorney to review and evaluate. That attorney's job is to point out all of the consequences of executing the agreement to his/her client, or suggest alternative provisions that might be more beneficial. When someone is in love and eager to marry, he/she doesn't necessarily think about the "what if" scenario of divorce. The attorney must also discuss the implications of the death of one or both of the spouses, as many agreements also have terms that deal with the disposition of property in the event of the death of one or both of the spouses.

It is not unusual for the attorneys to negotiate the terms over the span of several months. It is important to be prepared well before the wedding to give everyone ample time to negotiate and prepare required financial disclosures. Finally, attorneys assist in the execution of the agreement, often meeting with both parties to make sure the agreement is properly executed and all final terms are satisfactory.

17.6 My fiancé asked me to sign a prenuptial agreement the day before our wedding. I know nothing about his finances and signed the agreement without speaking with an attorney. Will this agreement be enforced?

Maybe. Prenuptial agreements are enforceable unless the party challenging the agreement can prove he/she did not enter into the agreement voluntarily. The question of whether someone was acting voluntarily depends upon a number of factors, including your receipt of a full financial disclosure from your fiancé and an opportunity to consult with an attorney. If you were not given a full disclosure, and didn't waive your right to a disclosure, you probably didn't enter into this agreement voluntarily. Don't ever sign an agreement without first consulting your own attorney to determine its effect on your future.

17.7 What other criteria makes a prenuptial agreement unenforceable?

Intent is at the heart of whether a prenuptial agreement is enforceable. If someone signed an agreement under duress, the agreement is not voluntary. If someone can prove he/she entered into the agreement under duress, meaning they were deprived of the exercise of free will, then it is likely unenforceable.

People have claimed duress based upon being presented an agreement on the eve of the wedding. That fact alone may not invalidate the agreement; however, it does raise some doubts. Other factors such as full disclosure and full legal representation will often be missing if the agreement is indeed presented at the door of the church. The person presented with a last-minute agreement may, of course, opt to cancel the wedding. However, people are often hesitant to cancel a wedding close to the event because they have already expended so much money on the wedding and have extended invitations to guests. To prove duress, one must show more than just bad taste, embarrassment, or annoyance. In addition to just showing that the wedding had already been planned and money spent, one would also likely be able to demonstrate that given the close proximity to the wedding, they were prevented from adequate disclosure of finances and from proper representation.

Agreements may also be considered "unconscionable" at the time they are executed and these are also unenforceable. An *unconscionable agreement* is one that is outrageous or oppressive. A judge will consider all the circumstances at the time the agreement was made to determine if the agreement is unconscionable. The lack of full disclosure may cause an agreement to be unconscionable if the parties didn't waive full disclosure in the agreement. If there is a waiver, but only one person had representation, this could be unconscionable. It all depends on the complete circumstances. For this reason, it is critical to always have legal representation on both sides.

17.8 I waited to the last minute and didn't have time to do the prenuptial agreement. Can I do one after I get married?

It is possible to create an agreement called a postnuptial agreement, as described previously. New Mexico has a statute that specifically authorizes spouses to enter into agreements or contracts with each other and the "consideration" can be only an exchange of mutual promises. However, for postnuptial agreements, the same criteria as for a prenuptial agreement of fairness, full disclosure, and legal representation for both parties is essential to ensure enforceability. As a practical matter, once you are married, your spouse has little incentive to agree to a postnuptial agreement. You may need to add some actual consideration, such as the transfer of property or funds, to the other spouse in exchange for the agreement that is sought to reach a voluntary, fair agreement. Again, the importance of having both spouses fully represented and there being full and complete disclosure cannot be emphasized enough.

In Closing

Now, pause and breathe. Acknowledge yourself for the courage you have shown in examining your unique situation, needs, and goals. You are facing your future and recasting yourself into a new life. You are looking more closely at your living situation, the needs of your children, your financial security, and your personal growth and healing. You are seeing your situation and acknowledging the truth about what you now need. You are taking action to propel you into new possibilities.

From here, it is time to take inventory of the lessons learned, goals met, and actions yet to take. Celebrate each of those steps forward and be gentle with yourself over the occasional misstep backward. You have transitioned through this time when everything is reduced to the core of you. Gone are the familiar habits of your marriage. With every day moving closer to the completion of your divorce, your grief will begin to subside and your energy improve as you move toward a fresh start. All the best to you as you accomplish this life journey.

Resources

Annual Credit Report Request Service
P.O. Box 105283
Atlanta, GA 30348-5283
(877) 322-8228
www.AnnualCreditReport.com

This website offers a centralized service for consumers to request annual credit reports. It was created by the three nationwide consumer credit reporting companies: Equifax, Experian, and TransUnion. AnnualCreditReport.com processes requests for free credit file disclosures (commonly called credit reports). Under the *Fair and Accurate Credit Transactions Act (FACT Act)*, consumers can request and obtain a free credit report once every twelve months from each of the three nationwide consumer credit reporting companies. AnnualCreditReport.com offers consumers a fast and convenient way to request, view, and print their credit reports in a secure Internet environment. It also provides options to request reports by telephone and by mail.

Internal Revenue Service (IRS)
(800) 829-1040 tax assistance for individual tax questions or
(800) 829-4933 for business tax questions.
www.irs.gov

The IRS website allows you to search for any key word, review publications and information on tax questions, or submit a question via e-mail or phone to an IRS representative.

New Mexico Coalition Against Domestic Violence (NMCADV)
1210 Luisa Street, Suite 7
Santa Fe, NM 87505
(505) 246-9240
www.nmcadv.org

The New Mexico Coalition Against Domestic Violence is a state-wide advocacy organization committed to the prevention and elimination of sexual and domestic violence. NMCADVworks to enhance safety and justice for victims of domestic violence and sexual assault by supporting and building upon the services provided by the network of local programs.

New Mexico Crisis and Access Line (NMCAL)
(855) 662-7474
www.nmcrisisline.com

NMCAL helps New Mexicans get immediate access to local help and resources during a mental health crisis. It is staffed by master's-level clinicians who can respond to a crisis 24 hours per day and 7 days per week.

New Mexico Child Support Enforcement Division (CSED)
(800) 288-7207
Toll-free (800) 585-7631 outside of New Mexico
www.hsd.state.nm.us/csed/
www.hsd.state.nm.us/Child_Support_Enforcement_Division.aspx
www.hsd.state.nm.us/LookingForAssistance/Child_Support.aspx

The Child Support Enforcement Program helps children obtain financial support from both parents, enables current public assistance recipients to end their reliance on welfare, and can help prevent single parents from entering public assistance.

New Mexico Legal Aid
301 Gold Ave. SW
P.O. Box 25486
Albuquerque, NM 87125
(505) 243-7871
Toll-free (866) 416-1922
www.nmlegalaid.org

The mission of New Mexico Legal Aid is to promote justice, dignity, hope, and self-sufficiency through quality civil legal services for those who have nowhere else to turn. Legal Aid provides referral, advice, brief service, and placement for extended representation with local offices across the state.

New Mexico Legal Aid
Domestic Violence/Sexual Assault/Stalking
Help Line: (877) 974-3400
www.lawhelpnewmexico.org
Provides legal information and referrals for victims of domestic violence, sexual assault, and stalking.

New Mexico Second Judicial District Court
400 Lomas NW
Albuquerque, NM 87102
(505) 841-8400
www.nmcourts.gov/seconddistrictcourt

State Bar of New Mexico General Referral Program
(505) 797-6066 or (800) 876-6227
www.nmbar.org/Nmstatebar/For_Public/Lawyer_Referral.aspx
The State Bar General Referral Program assists those who need legal help but are unsure where to find it. The program can put you in contact with a private attorney for up to 30 minutes of legal consultation/case assessment for a cost of a $35 referral fee.

Social Security Administration
Office of Public Inquiries
6401 Security Boulevard
Baltimore, MD 21235
(800) 772-1213
www.ssa.gov
The website enables users to search for a question or word, submit questions via e-mail, or review recent publications.

UNM School of Law Clinical Program
1117 Stanford NE MSC 11 6070
1 University of New Mexico
Albuquerque, NM 87131-0001
(505) 277-2146
http://lawschool.unm.edu/clinic/index.php
One of the first law schools in the country to create a mandatory clinic, UNM also pioneered the use of technology in the clinical program with the development and use of an automated case management system. Constantly expanding and evolving, UNM's clinical program continues to be recognized as a national leader.

The Volunteer Attorneys Project (VAP)

301 Gold Avenue, SW
P.O. Box 25486
Albuquerque, NM 87104
(505) 768-6114
www.probono.net/oppsguide/organization.135709-New_Mexico_
Legal_Aid_Volunteer_Attorney_Program

The VAP is a statewide volunteer legal services project and referral network founded on the belief that all citizens should have access to the legal system, regardless of ability to pay.

Other Recommended Websites

Up to Parents

www.uptoparents.org

A free, confidential, and interactive website for divorcing and divorced parents.

The American Bar Association

www.americanbar.org/groups/family_law/resources.html
Legal resources and client manuals are available online.

Academy of Matrimonial Attorneys

www.aaml.org/information-center

The AMML's website features an information center with links to information on alimony, enforcement of property division, pets, tax issues, adoption, third-party rights regarding children.

International Academy of Collaborative Professionals

www.collaborativepractice.com

The International Academy of Collaborative Professionals is an international community of legal, mental health, and financial professionals working in concert to create client-centered processes for resolving conflict.

Glossary

Affidavit: A written statement of facts made under oath and signed before a notary public. Affidavits are used primarily when there will not be a hearing in open court with live testimony. The attorney will prepare an affidavit to present relevant facts. Affidavits may be signed by the parties or in some cases by witnesses. The person signing the affidavit may be referred to as the *affiant.*

Alimony: Court-ordered spousal support payments from one party to another, often to enable the recipient spouse to become economically independent.

Allegation: A statement that one party claims is true.

Answer: A written response to the petition for dissolution of marriage. It serves to admit or deny the allegations therein and may also make claims against the opposing party. An answer should be filed within thirty days of either (a) the complaint being served by the sheriff or (b) the respondent's voluntary appearance being filed with the court.

Appeal: The process by which a higher court reviews the decision of a lower court. In New Mexico family law cases, a person will first file an appeal with the New Mexico Court of Appeals. After that appeal is decided there may be a further appeal to the New Mexico Supreme Court.

Application for removal of jurisdiction: A parent's written request to the court seeking permission to relocate to another state with the children.

Application to modify: A party's written request to the court to change a prior order regarding custody, child support, alimony, or any other order that the court may change by law.

Child support: Financial support for a child paid by the noncustodial parent to the custodial parent.

Contempt of court: The willful and intentional failure of a party to comply with a court order, judgment, or decree. Contempt may be punishable by a fine or jail.

Contested case: Any case in which the parties cannot reach an agreement. A contested case will result in a trial to have the judge decide disputed issues.

Court order: A court-issued document setting forth the judge's orders. An order can be issued based upon the parties' agreement or the judge's decision. An order may require the parties to perform certain acts or set forth their rights and responsibilities. An order is put in writing, signed by the judge, and filed with the court.

Court order acceptable for processing (COAP): A type of court order that provides for payment of civil service retirement to a former spouse.

Cross-examination: The questioning of a witness by the opposing counsel during trial or at a deposition, in response to questions asked by the other attorney.

Custody: The legal right and responsibility awarded by a court for the possession of, care of, and decision making for a minor child.

Decree: The final order entered in a divorce.

Deposition: A witness's testimony taken out of court, under oath, and in the presence of attorneys and a court reporter. If a person gives a different testimony at the time of trial, he/she can be impeached with the deposition testimony; that is, statements made at a deposition can be used to show untruthfulness if a different answer is given at trial.

Direct examination: The initial questioning of a witness in court by the attorney who called him or her to the stand.

Discovery: A process used by attorneys to discover information from the opposing party for the purpose of fully assessing a case for settlement or trial. Types of discovery include interrogatories, requests for production of documents, and requests for admissions.

Dissolution: The act of terminating or dissolving a marriage.

Glossary

Equitable distribution of property: The method by which real and personal property and debts are divided in a divorce. Given all economic circumstances of the parties, New Mexico law requires that marital property and debts be divided in a fair and reasonable manner.

Ex parte: Usually in reference to a motion, the term used to describe an appearance of only one party before the judge, without the other party being present. For example, an *ex parte* restraining order may be granted immediately after the filing of a complaint for divorce.

Final decree of dissolution of marriage: A final court order dissolving the marriage, dividing property and debts, ordering support, and entering other orders regarding finances and the minor children.

Guardian *ad litem* (GAL): A person, often an attorney or mental health professional, appointed by court to conduct an investigation regarding the children's best interest.

Hearing: Any proceeding before the court for the purpose of resolving disputed issues between the parties through presentation of testimony, affidavits, exhibits, or argument.

Hold-harmless clause: A term in a court order that requires one party to assume responsibility for a debt and to protect the other spouse from any loss or expense in connection with it, as in to hold harmless from liability.

Interrogatories: Written questions sent from one party to the other that are used to obtain facts or opinions related to the divorce.

Joint custody: The shared right and responsibility of both parents awarded by the court for possession, care, and decision making for children.

Jurisdiction: The authority of a court to make rulings affecting a party.

Mediation: A process by which a neutral third party facilitates negotiations between the parties on a wide range of issues.

Motion: A written application to the court for relief, such as temporary child support, custody, or restraining orders.

No-fault divorce: The type of divorce New Mexico has that does not require evidence of marital misconduct. This means that abandonment, cruelty, and adultery are neither relevant nor required to be proven for the purposes of granting the divorce.

Notice of hearing: A written statement sent to the opposing attorney or spouse listing the date and place of a hearing and the nature of the matters that will be heard by the court. In New Mexico, one party is required to give the other party reasonable notice of any court hearing.

Party: The person in a legal action whose rights or interests will be affected by the divorce. For example, in a divorce the parties include the two spouses.

Pending: During the case. For example, the judge may award you temporary support while your case is pending.

Petitioner: A term used to refer to the plaintiff or person who files the complaint seeking a divorce.

Petition for dissolution of marriage: The first document filed with the clerk of the court in an action for divorce, separation, or paternity. The complaint sets forth the facts on which the requested relief is based.

Pleadings: Documents filed with the court seeking a court order.

Qualified domestic relations order (QDRO): A type of court order that provides for direct payment from a retirement account to a former spouse.

Qualified medical support order (QMSO): A type of court order that provides a former spouse certain rights regarding medical insurance and information.

Request for production of documents: A written request for documents sent from one party to the other during the discovery process.

Respondent: The responding party to a divorce; the party who did not file the complaint initiating the divorce.

Sequester: To order prospective witnesses out of the courtroom until they have concluded giving their testimony.

Service: The process of notifying a party about a legal filing.

Setoff: A debt or financial obligation of one spouse that is deducted from the debt or financial obligation of the other spouse.

Settlement: The agreed resolution of disputed issues.

Show cause: Written application to the court to hold another person in contempt of court for violating or failing to comply with a current court order.

Stipulation: An agreement reached between parties or an agreement by their attorneys.

Glossary

Subpoena: A document delivered to a person or witness that requires him or her to appear in court, appear for a deposition, or produce documents. Failure to comply could result in punishment by the court. A subpoena requesting documents is called a *subpoena duces tecum.*

Temporary order of protection (TOP): An order of the court prohibiting a party from certain behavior. For example, a temporary restraining order may order a person not to transfer any funds during a pending divorce action.

Trial: A formal court hearing in which the judge will decide disputed issues raised by the parties' pleadings.

Under advisement: A term used to describe the status of a case, usually after a court hearing on a motion or a trial, when the judge has not yet made a decision.

Index

Index

Index

tion
  attorney's role in, 88
  benefits of, 80–82
  defined, 86
  phone calls and letters *vs.*, 87
  preparing for, 87
  spouse's attendance to, 26–27
  steps in, 88
settlement facilitators, 57–58
sexual orientation, 109
shame, 26
shared physical custody, 102
shuttling negotiations, 26–27
significant other, 133, 146
single tax filing status, 189
Social Security, 177
Social Security Administration (SSA), 177
sole legal custody, 102
sole physical custody, 112
special master, 41
sperm, 170
spousal support, 139–148
  accuracy of records of, 144
  affair and, 143
  bankruptcy and, 148
  college education and, 160
  death and, 146
  factors determining eligibility for, 141–142
  information for, 142–143
  length of time for receiving, 146
  modifying, 147–148
  nonmodifiable, 147–148
  out-of-state relocation and, 147
  payments for, 145
  permanent, 140–141
  property division *vs.*, 145
  reason for paying, 142
  refusal to pay, 147

  remarriage and, 146
  significant other and, 146
  spouse's income, proving real, 143–144
  taxes on, 144–145, 187–189
  types of, 140–141
  waiving, 148
spouse
  abuse by, 90–93, 97, 116
  agreement for divorce, 7
  amicable divorce with, 16–17
  anger and, 94–95
  arguing with, 117–118
  artificial reproduction and, 170
  attorney fees, responsibility for, 61
  child support, refusal to pay, 134
  college degree of, 160
  communicating with, 117–118
  court, attendance in, 196, 203
  debts, division of, 185
  "Disneyland parent" behavior of, 22–23
  documentation from, 16
  domestic violence by, 91–93, 116–117
  emptying of bank accounts by, 95–96
  fearing your (*see* emergency)
  fighting with, 117–118
  financial information from, 16
  income, proving real, 143–144
  infidelity by, 6–7
  locating, 8
  loving feelings towards, 24–25

About the Authors

Sandra Morgan Little, a New Mexico native and cofounder of Little, Gilman-Tepper and Batley, P.A., has focused her practice on representing high-net-worth individuals, business owners, CEOs, and their spouses. Sandra has been involved in some of the largest family cases in New Mexico. She has tried hundreds of cases in various courts across New Mexico and nine of her cases have been reported by the New Mexico Supreme Court. Sandra frequently involves accountants, business lawyers, and other financial experts in cases to provide avenues for protecting and maintaining wealth and businesses.

Sandra served as chair of the American Bar Association Family Law Section, the world's largest family law organization, and is a diplomate of the American College of Family Trial Attorneys which recognizes the top 100 family law litigators in the country. She has been listed in *Best Lawyers in America* for more than twenty-five years and was named the Family Lawyer of the Year by *Best Lawyers* the first time the award was given. She has been selected as a Southwest Super Lawyer since its inception and was selected as one of the Top 25 Lawyers in New Mexico. She has been a fellow of the prestigious American Academy of Matrimonial Lawyers for thirty years and is a New Mexico certified family law specialist.

A prolific writer and speaker, Sandra has lectured to thousands of attorneys across the country on various family law topics primarily focused on business valuation in divorce, representing high-net-worth individuals, retirement in divorce, and using experts in settlement and trial. She has been quoted as an expert on divorce in a number of publications including *The Wall Street Journal, Newsweek, Fortune, The New York Times, Glamour,* and *Martha Stewart Living.* Sandra may be reached at **www.lgtfamilylaw.com.**

Jan Gilman-Tepper, a New Mexico native and firm cofounder, has practiced family law exclusively for more than thirty years. She concentrates her practice in the area of business and high-net-worth divorces. Her clients have included entertainers, professional athletes, and business owners, or their spouses.

Ms. Gilman-Tepper frequently lectures on collaborative and litigation divorce topics for continuing legal education seminars in New Mexico for other attorneys, and for financial and mental health professionals. She has lectured on such topics as the collaborative divorce process, complex litigation in divorce, trial practice, business valuations, and professionalism.

Jan is often involved in multi-layered or multi-jurisdictional cases that involve business valuations, professional goodwill, multi-state business organizations, prenuptial agreements, and tax issues.

Ms. Gilman-Tepper has written for the prestigious *American Academy of Matrimonial Lawyers Journal* and is certified as a *family law specialist* by both the American Academy of Matrimonial Lawyers and the New Mexico Board of Specialization. She has been listed in Martindale-Hubbell's Bar Register of Preeminent Lawyers every year since 1997, *Best Lawyers in America* every year since 1987, and as a Southwest Super Lawyer every year since 2007. She is also a fellow in the American Academy of Matrimonial Lawyers. Jan may be reached at: **www.lgtfamilylaw.com.**

Roberta "Bobbie" Batley was born and raised in Farmington, New Mexico, and grew up in a family business. Bobbie has practiced family law for almost twenty years and is a New Mexico board-recognized specialist in divorce and family law. Bobbie represents clients in a variety of family law cases, often involving complex matrimonial and property division issues including business valuation, professional goodwill, and multi-state and multi-layered business structures. In addition, she handles prenuptial and postnuptial agreements, child-custody, and child-support cases.

Bobbie feels that her greatest strength is guiding her clients through one of the most difficult times in their lives to reach a better emotional and financial platform postdivorce. She wants her clients to understand the options available to them to address their family law matter in and out of the court system. Bobbie is a skilled trial lawyer and has tried cases of all levels in courts throughout New Mexico. She also is aware that litigation may not always be the best option for resolving a family law case. Bobbie offers advanced collaborative techniques and interest-based negotiation skills to help her clients address their family law matters without court involvement if that is their goal. Further, Bobbie serves for both the court and her colleagues as a settlement facilitator in family law matters.

Bobbie is the current secretary of the American Bar Association Family Law Section, representing family law attorneys across the country. She is also a fellow of the American Academy of Matrimonial Lawyers. In 2012, she was named by *Best Lawyers in America* as the New Mexico Family Law Lawyer of the Year and has been listed in that publication since 2006. She has been named as a Southwest Super Lawyer since 2010, and is also recognized by Martindale-Hubbell as a "pre-eminent woman lawyer." In addition, Bobbie serves on the advisory board of the Honoring Families Initiative of the Institute for the Advancement of the American Legal System (IAALS). IAALS is dedicated to facilitating continuous improvement and advancing excellence in the American legal system.

In New Mexico, Bobbie remains an active member of the New Mexico Family Law Section of the State Bar, the New Mexico Collaborative Practice Group, and the Albuquerque Collaborative Practice Group. She is also a member of the Future Fund of the Albuquerque Community Foundation and a Leadership New Mexico Connect Program Graduate. Bobbie can be reached at **www.lgtfamilylaw.com.**

Tiffany Oliver Leigh is a board-certified family law specialist and former chair of the Family Law Section of the State Bar of New Mexico. Tiffany is dedicated to the education of both family law attorneys and litigants. She has served for many years as the chair of the New Mexico Family Law Institute and the New Mexico Collaborative Symposium. Tiffany is a founder and regular volunteer at the Divorce Options Workshop, a monthly community outreach program designed to teach *pro se* litigants how to resolve their family law issues without the need for court intervention. Tiffany frequently presents at continuing education seminars and in 2011 received the Continuing Legal Education Crest Award, an award given to the top young lawyer presentation by the State Bar of New Mexico.

Tiffany's practice is focused on a wide array of family law cases including complex divorce cases involving business valuation, property division, child custody, child support, and pre/postnuptial agreements. She is a skilled negotiator who seeks creative solutions both inside and outside the courtroom.

Tiffany has been recognized as a Southwest Super Lawyers Rising Star in both 2014 and 2015, a distinction bestowed upon only 2.5 percent of the licensed active attorneys in the state. In 2014, Tiffany coauthored an amicus brief which resulted in the New Mexico Supreme Court reversing a Court of Appeals decision and extending guardians *ad litem* quasi-judicial immunity.

Tiffany is called upon regularly by the court to serve as a settlement facilitator in all types of family law cases. She is also the chair of the Board of Directors of Wesley Kids, an outreach of the First United Methodist Church.

In April of 2015, Tiffany started her own office and can be reached at **www.ldfamilylaw.com.**

Divorce Titles from Addicus Books

Visit our online catalog at www.AddicusBooks.com

Divorce in Alabama: The Legal Process, Your Rights, and What to Expect $21.95

Divorce in Arizona: The Legal Process, Your Rights, and What to Expect. $21.95

Divorce in California: The Legal Process, Your Rights, and What to Expect $21.95

Divorce in Connecticut: The Legal Process, Your Rights, and What to Expect $21.95

Divorce in Florida: The Legal Process, Your Rights, and What to Expect $21.95

Divorce in Georgia: Simple Answers to Your Legal Questions $21.95

Divorce in Hawaii: The Legal Process, Your Rights, and What to Expect $21.95

Divorce in Illinois: The Legal Process, Your Rights, and What to Expect $21.95

Divorce in Louisiana: The Legal Process, Your Rights, and What to Expect $21.95

Divorce in Maine: The Legal Process, Your Rights, and What to Expect $21.95

Divorce in Michigan: The Legal Process, Your Rights, and What to Expect. $21.95

Divorce in Mississippi: The Legal Process, Your Rights, and What to Expect. $21.95

Divorce in Missouri: The Legal Process, Your Rights, and What to Expect $21.95

Divorce in Nebraska: The Legal Process, Your Rights, and What to Expect—2nd Edition $21.95

Divorce in Nevada: The Legal Process, Your Rights, and What to Expect. $21.95

Divorce in New Jersey: The Legal Process, Your Rights, and What to Expect $21.95

Divorce in New York: The Legal Process, Your Rights, and What to Expect $21.95

Divorce in North Carolina: The Legal Process, Your Rights, and What to Expect $21.95

Divorce in Tennessee: The Legal Process, Your Rights, and What to Expect $21.95

Divorce in Virginia: The Legal Process, Your Rights, and What to Expect $21.95

Divorce in Washington: The Legal Process, Your Rights, and What to Expect $21.95

Divorce in West Virginia: The Legal Process, Your Rights, and What to Expect $21.95

Divorce in Wisconsin: The Legal Process, Your Rights, and What to Expect $21.95

To Order Books:
Visit us online at: www.AddicusBooks.com
Call toll free: (800) 888-4741

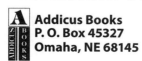

Addicus Books
P. O. Box 45327
Omaha, NE 68145